Barbara T. Mates

Adaptive Technology for the Internet

Making Electronic Resources Accessible to All

with contributions by
DOUG WAKEFIELD and
JUDITH DIXON

AMERICAN LIBRARY ASSOCIATION
Chicago and London 2000

Trademarked names appear in the text of this book. Rather than identify or insert a trademark symbol at the appearance of each name, the authors and the American Library Association state that the names are used for editorial purposes exclusively, to the ultimate benefit of the owners of the trademarks. There is absolutely no intention of infringement on the rights of the trademark owners. Inclusion of a vendor or product in this book does not constitute or imply endorsement or certification by the American Library Association.

Project editor: Joan McLaughlin

Text designer: Dianne M. Rooney

Composition by BookComp in Caxton Light and Univers using TEX

Printed on 50-pound white offset, a pH-neutral stock, and bound in 10-point coated cover stock by Documation

The paper used in this publication meets the minimum requirements of American National Standard for Information Sciences—Permanence of Paper for Printed Library Materials, ANSI Z39.48-1992. ♾

Library of Congress Cataloging-in-Publication Data

Mates, Barbara T.

Adaptive technology for the Internet : making electronic resources accessible to all / Barbara T. Mates ; with contributions by Doug Wakefield and Judith Dixon.

p. cm.

Includes index.

ISBN 0-8389-0752-0

1. Libraries and the blind—United States. 2. Libraries and the handicapped—United States. 3. Libraries—United States—Special collections—Computer network resources. 4. Blind, Apparatus for the—United States. 5. Adaptive computing—United States. I. Wakefield, Doug. II. Dixon, Judith M. III. Title.

Z675.B M38 1999

027.6'63—dc21 98-31936

Printed in the United States of America

04 03 02 01 00 5 4 3 2 1

This work is once again dedicated to my parents, Ann and the late Tony, and to my husband, James.

It is also dedicated to my friends and loved ones, both here and away.

Thanks for always having confidence in me and standing by me.

For people without disabilities, technology makes things convenient, whereas for people with disabilities, it makes things possible . . . [this] fact brings with it an enormous responsibility because the reverse is also true. Inaccessible technology can make things absolutely impossible for disabled people, a prospect we must avoid.

—Judith Heumann, Assistant Secretary
of the Office of Special Education
and Rehabilitative Services,
U.S. Department of Education

Keynote address to Microsoft employees
and experts on disabilities and technology,
Redmond, Washington, February 19, 1998

Contents

Appendixes

Preface

It has become fashionable for libraries, like corporations, to develop mission statements or vision statements that will guide them in delivering state-of-the-art services to their patrons.

Frequently a phrase such as "equal access to information through technology" is included in one or both statements. Often forgotten in these plans, however, are accommodations for persons with disabilities who need to access information using adaptive technology.

"The 1997 National Survey of U.S. Public Libraries and the Internet," commissioned by the American Library Association (ALA), Office for Information Technology, found few libraries actually provide special software or hardware for persons with disabilities. While urban areas offered the most adapted access to hardware and software, only 15.4 percent of those responding indicated that they have made access accommodations to their automated information systems.[1] This figure is unacceptable for entities that profess to be citadels of knowledge, dedicated to "equal access" to information. In an age where quality information available via the Internet is growing, libraries should be seeking to ensure that their systems are accessible by everyone.

While the libraries that make up the network of the National Library Service (NLS) for the Blind and Physically Handicapped provide leisure reading for three-quarters of a million people, accessible, supplemental reference and ephemeral information is still lacking. This creates a discriminatory information gap between those who have access to information and those who do not. Librarians and Web masters can remedy the information gap by ensuring that the Websites they design are accessible to those using adaptive technology and that these librarians and Web masters purchase equipment and software that will facilitate this access.

As the Regional Librarian for the Blind and Physically Handicapped at the Cleveland Public Library, I see the growing need for computer access by the population we serve. More patrons are acquiring adaptive technology for home use and are anxious to "get on the information highway." Other patrons, curious about the Internet but lacking funds to purchase their own equipment, are seeking public environments to access the Internet.

This work seeks to guide information providers in establishing accessible Websites and acquiring the hardware and software needed by people with disabilities. The book focuses on access to the Internet using large print, voice, and Braille. Contributors Judith Dixon and Doug Wakefield are respected experts in the field of adaptive technology and the Internet. Both have lectured widely on the subject and use adaptive technology extensively. In this book, we describe specific products. Fortunately, new adaptive technologies are continually being developed. What we describe here is a snapshot of development at this writing. You should read these product descriptions as examples of a class of products. Use such resources as the Websites recommended in the book or in Appendix 2, "Selected Vendors, Manufacturers, and Consultants," to keep up with the latest developments.

The reader will also learn how to acquire the funds for adaptive technology, what type of equipment to choose, where to purchase the equipment, and how to inform the community of your progress. Tips for ensuring that the equipment is placed in a nurturing environment are also included. Additionally, the book will direct the reader to useful Websites and to libraries that are in various stages of providing library access to persons with disabilities.

It is my hope that this book will help librarians and information providers add substance to the language in mission statements concerning persons with disabilities. Technology has the promise of aiding everyone; the information explosion should not be limited to the "temporally abled."

Note

1. J. C. Bertot, C. R. McClure, and P. D. Fletcher, "The 1997 National Survey of U.S. Public Libraries and the Internet: Final Report" (Washington, D.C.: American Library Association, Office for Information Technology Policy, 1997). Available at <www.research.umbc.edu/~bertot/ala.97>.

Acknowledgments

The author acknowledges that without the help of colleagues (known and unknown) this work would not have been possible. Therefore she would like to say "thanks again" to a few of them.

Judy and Doug, thanks for always saying "yes" to requests for sharing your vast knowledge of adaptive technology with us novices. We will try to pass it on.

James, thanks for doing all the charts with less-than-coherent directions from myself.

Rocky and Dessie, thanks for sending all the equipment pictures to me; it saved me precious time.

To all my colleagues who are making their libraries and information accessible, thank you for leading the way. A special thank you to those of you who took the time to fill out my survey; your contributions helped form a very important part of this book and serve as examples of what is possible. An extra special "thank you" to Audrey Gorman for her contribution on access for patrons with learning disabilities.

To the Website managers at "DO-IT," WebABLE!, ATRC (Toronto), Trace, EASI, CPB/WGBH, CAST, LC/NLS, WAI, Sun Microsystems, Disabilities Resources, Inc., Closing the Gap, Inc., Cleveland Public Library, and other quality Websites, my eternal gratitude. Without your efforts in creating information-rich Websites, this work would not have been possible.

Lastly, thanks to Patrick Hogan, Editorial Director for ALA Editions, for asking "if I'd like to write a book," as well as Mary Huchting for her understanding and Joan McLaughlin who fixed the "grammar." Thanks to Dianne Rooney for her artistic flair.

1

Could Helen Keller Use Your Library?

It is estimated that in the United States alone, there are 12 million visually impaired persons plus 39 million learning disabled persons who cannot access printed materials because of their disabilities. Additionally, 11.7 million physically disabled people also perceive the format of books and paper as obstructions to information access, for they cannot hold a book or turn a sheet of paper.

The access problem people with disabilities encounter with printed books applies to all printed materials, including items such as informational fliers, newspapers, general correspondence, and information found via standard computer access.

Persons who are visually impaired or learning disabled must use another sense (hearing or touch) to read printed text. People with physical impairments must find a way to manipulate the format of the text or their ability to learn will be limited to the one "page" of information they can see.

All people with disabilities must be allowed equal access to information. If they do not have equal access to information, they will not receive an education that will allow them to thrive in a competitive society.

Limitations of Special Libraries

Previous to the passage of the Americans with Disabilities Act (ADA) and an overall price decrease in the cost of basic computers and software, the solution most of the library world used when approached by patrons with print disabilities seeking information was to refer them to "special libraries," for example, the National Library Services (NLS) for the Blind and Physically Handicapped or Recordings for the Blind and Dyslexic (RFB&D).[1] Another solution was to ask, "Well, why don't you ask a friend or neighbor to read it for you?"

While the suggestion of referring the patron to the NLS or the RFB&D for books is indeed commendable, it is too limiting. Both organizations pride themselves on their holdings, but they cannot keep pace with the publishing world. Of the 40,000 books published annually, the NLS is able to add only 2,000, while public libraries serving a similar-size population purchase 31,420 titles.[2] The 2,000 titles the NLS chooses must fill the needs of patrons from the ages of one to 101, while attempting to meet the informational needs of all patrons at all times of their lives. This means the number of titles available on any subject or genre is going to be extremely limited. The NLS is also very careful not to produce titles whose information is time-sensitive and likely to be out-of-date soon after the production of the book, or local histories, or items of limited interests. This means that pop culture and current trends do not receive much coverage, and the acquisition of ready reference materials is nonexistent.

In addition to not being able to have an in-depth collection, another problem encountered when referring persons with disabilities to the NLS is that many of these libraries are remotely located in respect to the patron's neighborhood. Thus, the disabled person would have to find a way to get to the library with the books or the adapted technology.

While it is still economically necessary to refer disabled patrons to the NLS libraries for the bulk of their recreational reading materials, all libraries with computers and Internet access can provide gateways to sites with complete texts as well as community bulletin-board information, in addition to current information such as newspapers and magazines.

As for asking a friend or neighbor to read the material, this would be akin to producing an informational flier in Mandarin and, when asked for an English version, saying, "Sorry, I cannot give you one; however, a computer will translate the words on the flier, but I am afraid it is located at a library 100 miles away."

Thinking beyond Budgets

Although technology has become easier to use and less expensive, many libraries still take the referral approach to patrons with disabilities. They see their budgets shrinking and feel adapting their library equipment and their collections is nonprudent, for "persons with disabilities do not use their library." If they were to reevaluate the thought process that brought them to such a conclusion, however, they would find a way to budget funds for information access.

What adaptive devices would you purchase if it were possible for Helen Keller, Albert Einstein, Robert Louis Stevenson, or Pierre-Auguste Renoir to be born again into the community you serve and become a library patron? What modifications would you make to your Website if you knew that Stephen Hawking or Christopher Reeve were accessing it? "Whatever it takes" is the answer most information providers would give, for these people are known to be valued contributors to our society, and they have a constant need to access information.

New Possibilities through Computing

By now most information providers have formed rather strong opinions about the Internet. The Internet is the actual interconnectivity of computer-based information resources around the world. A variety of methods facilitate communications between these computer systems. Electronic mail is one of the most popular ways for individuals and businesses to use the Internet. Those who love the Internet do so because of all the information that can accessed; those who hate it, hate it because in addition to all the useful information found on the highway there are detours of inaccurate information, chat rooms, and noninformation. For librarians and information specialists who are aware of the lack of accessible information for readers who are print impaired, however, the Internet coupled with adaptive technology is as important as the invention of the printing press.

People with disabilities but with access to computers equipped with adaptive technology can independently find and access information. Software programs can increase the size of the printed word so much that the person with a severe visual impairment can read what is on the screen. Screen readers read aloud with voice synthesizers text displayed on the computer screen, making it accessible to people who are blind and visually impaired as well as some learning disabled people with dyslexia. Mouse and keyboard simulators allow persons whose mobility is limited to one finger to cruise the Internet. And special switches allow patrons who can control minimal voluntary muscles (e.g., mouth, eye, foot) to keep current with the world around them.

Librarians and information specialists must help to make the Internet accessible to all. They can do this by first making sure their Website is accessible; second, they can be sure that they have adaptive computers available in accessible locations. Additionally, they should avoid subscribing to commercial sites that present obstacles to patrons using adaptive computer equipment. Who would pay to access a cardiology database written only with cuneiform? Why pay for databases that screen readers can't access?

"Curb Cuts" in the Information Superhighway

Many people in the electronic communication industry agree with the need for access for all by all, and they are refusing to buy nonaccessible computer products. Larry Goldberg, Director of Media Access, National Center for Accessible Media (NCAM), expressed the need for "curb cuts" in cyberspace and pointed out that the users are the only ones who can make the demand known.[3] Windows 95, for instance, was released with more access features for visually impaired users than ever anticipated or hoped for. Goldberg believes that five new employees were hired to create access because the state of Massachusetts and the federal government told Microsoft that Massachusetts and the federal government would not be able to purchase the new operating system for their hundreds of thousands of employees because of laws requiring equal access in the public workplace. The added features offer all users of Windows 95 a multitude of input and output alternatives for a broad range of users, not just the disabled.

Microsoft's owner, Bill Gates, admitted that today's most powerful software is becoming more graphics oriented and that the World Wide Web (WWW) is threatening to become less accessible to the blind. He stated that Microsoft was developing and would soon release technology designed to make it easy for authors and third parties to add closed-captioning and audio description to Web pages and software applications.[4]

The World Wide Web Consortium (W3C) launched an International Program Office for Web Accessibility in the fall of 1997. It has received funding from the Department of Education and the National Science Foundation (NSF). President Clinton endorsed the venture by stating, "The Web has the potential to be one of technology's greatest creators of opportunity, bringing the resources of the world directly to all people, but this can only be done if the Web is designed in a way that enables everyone to use it."[5]

Designing Libraries for Universal Access

Universal design is simply designing and acquiring services, buildings, materials, and equipment that can be used by a wide range of the population with various abilities and disabilities. Libraries have the ability to make the right choices when building their physical and virtual sites and for ensuring that all people will be able to use their facilities.

Demanding access for all library users makes sense morally and financially. With all the hype relating to digital media, an even greater need exists for a universally designed "Everyone Interface," for all forms of storing and transmitting digital media are not accessible by readers who are print impaired. We must all be careful that our equipment will have enough speed to access and retrieve the information we request. For example, an image or sound clip may take minutes to receive and download while the text version takes only seconds. The image or sound clip, however, would be usable by people who were unable to hear or see and would be accessible to the people and libraries who are unable to purchase new computers every year.

Taking Chances

Assistive technology is still frequently seen as an extra burden and extra expense. Generally, libraries have relegated the purchase and replacement of adaptive equipment to the realm of grants and gifts. They seldom spend money from the general fund on anything that's perceived as an added service or a frill.

Part of this attitude is based on lack of knowledge about the current state of the art in assistive technology. Part is from an erroneous belief that such technology is dedicated to and usable by only small groups of users and is very expensive. Some is based on earlier, more cumbersome technology and speculative, untested rationales for purchase that led to unused equipment gathering dust. And the rest comes from the impression that "it's not our responsibility" or that someone else is better equipped for the job.

It's true that not all assistive technology is used to the extent projected. That's also true of some books, journals, and other technology we invest in. We're not always right. With that admission out of the way, we can learn from our mistakes, learn from research, and continue to pursue service solutions for which we have good rationales.

Much assistive technology is now in software form, not confined to dedicated, single-function machines. Those do still exist for situations in which they're the best solution. The trend is toward off-the-shelf hardware and software that is designed to be adapted to the needs of many users. As with much technology, prices have fallen rapidly and continue to shrink. Slight added expense can be balanced against usefulness to more people.

The principle of universal design is being applied to make products and services available to the greatest number of people while taking diversity into account. Adaptations like the ability to increase font size and magnification are built in. Information is presented in redundant forms, covering a wide range of preferred learning styles and formats. Almost everybody can find some of the available features useful. The same features can spell the difference between information access and information poverty for those who truly need them.

"Access for all" is a phrase that is used a lot in the library world. Making information accessible to our communities is our job. If the phrase and the job are to be meaningful, we must discard outdated notions, take some chances, and make some mistakes. Whether Christopher Reeve or Helen Keller or Stephen Hawking use our services is irrelevant if we embrace the notion that we can and should give them access to what everyone else has. Whether the users we attract and serve become versed in quantum physics or physical fitness, we need to support their right to information. It's not only professionally and morally correct, it's the law. To disregard it is to really take chances.

Looking Ahead

Seniors also will be able to continue to access information. Many disabilities, such as the loss of vision, hearing, and the ability to flex one's hand, develop with age. In a world that is aging, one will see more people go from being "baby boomers" to "geri boomers"—remember, baby boomers are well educated and demanding and will want access to everything that there is. Having a working adaptive-technology plan in place will serve as a foundation for the new millennium.

Diversity in Adaptive Technology

Helen Keller was indeed a great person and an inspiration for everyone who has ever read her biography or watched a movie about her life and achievements; she was so great, in fact, she caused many people to learn incorrect information about the people who are blind and the people who are deaf.

Helen Keller was both blind and deaf, but most people with sensory disabilities are either blind (or visually impaired) or deaf (or hearing impaired). Basically, people who are deaf can (but not all do) read lips and print; many people who are hearing impaired do not know American Sign Language (ASL), but many people do. People who are blind can learn by auditory signals, but Braille is a writing medium of choice for many people with this type of disability. Many blind people do not know Braille and virtually none know ASL. Thus, no "one" piece of equipment will serve the needs of both the blind and the deaf populations. Understanding the manner in which each group as a whole intakes information will help with planning (as much as financially and practically as possible) for universal access.

Adaptions for Visual Impairments

The disability term *visual impairment* is broad in scope. It includes people who are color blind; people who have only peripheral vision; people who have only tunnel vision; people who cannot read standard print but can read large print. The commonality is that reading text on a computer screen is a challenge. Persons with usable vision will choose to access the computer visually rather than aurally.

Persons with visual impairments use a variety of adaptions to help them access information. All, however, require some type of screen-magnification hardware and software combination. A large monitor, for instance, will display text proportionally to the dimensions of the monitor; software programs, however, allow the user to enlarge the print if needed.

When designing a computer workstation for persons who are visually impaired, it may be helpful to use large-print keytops for the keyboard. Large-print keytops are a necessity for persons with visual impairments who never learned to type to learn how the keys of a standard QWERTY keyboard are laid out. Large-print keytops make it easier for everyone to "sneak a peek" at the keyboard, which increases the speed of inputting information.

Adaptions for Blindness

The disability term *blind* is sometimes used generically when talking about a group of people whose vision is severely impaired to the degree that they cannot receive any visual cues. They rely on auditory or tactile signals to access information.

When using computers, people who are blind may employ screen readers with speech synthesizers or Braille displays. The blind user utilizes keyboard navigation tools such as <TAB> and <ARROW> controls to move through menus, buttons, icons, text areas, and other parts of the graphic display to learn his or her position rather than a pointing device such as a mouse.[6] Without descriptive text or descriptions of illustrations and graphics, the blind user does not know what the object on the video display is.

When designing a computer workstation for patrons who are blind, it may be helpful to use tactile home-key markers or Braille keytops. The latter is useful for persons who never learned the QWERTY keyboard.

Adaptions for Mobility Impairments

The term *mobility impairment* is a general term that applies not only to persons who experience difficulty physically accessing a workstation or a keyboard or reading, but also to persons who have difficulty simultaneously pressing multiple keys of a computer (for example, <ALT-SHIFT-DEL>) or who lack the coordination to move a mouse and click the action button. This group of people would gain access to computers by using keyboard alternatives, mouse alternatives, and speech recognition through voice input. Many would also gain access through software that solves access problems.

A person with a mobility impairment may also be entering a facility via a wheelchair or a walker. This person would need a workstation that has the flexibility of height adjustment, which is useful for everyone, allowing a range of short and tall persons to comfortably use the workstation.

Adaptions for Hearing Impairments

The term *hearing impairment* is a general term that applies to persons who have difficulty discriminating changes in frequency or hearing certain frequencies. They may also have difficulties localizing sounds and differentiating background noises. Workstations for such users should be placed in areas with the least amount of distracting background noise, and headphones should be made available.

Persons with hearing impairments do not face many problems when using computers because of the minimal use of sound. As sound is added to Internet sites that are intended to reinforce a user action (i.e., chimes), however, visual data should be added. Software programs that translate auditory cues into visual cues on-screen also are helpful.

Large facilities should additionally be equipped with items such as Telecommunication Devices for the Deaf (TDD) Teletypewriters (TTYs), personal speech amplifiers (for example, pocket talkers), and visual alerting devices for emergency evacuations such as hand-lettered signs like BLIZZARD—CLOSING IN 15 MINUTES.

Adaptions for Deafness

Persons who are deaf have difficulty sensing any auditory cues. Like persons who are hearing impaired, they have few problems accessing the computer and the Internet. Software programs that caption auditory output are essential to the user, as are software programs that translate auditory beeps into visual displays.

Persons who are deaf also are helped by the same equipment as that supplied for the hearing impaired. Many people who are born deaf or become deaf early in life benefit from written instructions or sign language.

Adaptions for Learning Disabilities and Other Conditions That Affect Learning

Learning disabilities are neurological differences that can affect reading, writing, speaking and doing math. Specific learning disabilities differ from person to person, so individual needs must be taken into account. However, a few rules of thumb can improve access for the greatest number of people.

Whether dealing with online public access catalogs (OPACs), Web pages, or other information sources, contrast should be high and fonts simple for optimal readability. The ability to change font size, contrast, and colors is a must, but is now more common on standard software, particularly word processors. Consistent layout and clear navigation buttons with both graphic and text labels make navigation easier for everyone, but are essential for many people with disabilities. Background should be simple to improve readability and reduce distraction.

Directions should be broken down into steps and jargon avoided, including library jargon. White space and bulleting can clarify steps, reduce distraction, and focus attention. All graphics should have text alternatives or labels, which can be done in a variety of ways. This rule applies to computers and to signage throughout the facility.

Many people with moderate to severe reading disabilities, called dyslexia, benefit from optical character recognition and voice synthesizer software coupled with highlighting of the text being spoken. Using sight and sound together enhances speed and comprehension and may improve reading overall. Highlighting assists the user in keeping his or her place and following along. Adding a flatbed scanner ensures access to a wide variety of material not in electronic format.

People with a writing disability called dysgraphia are able to produce readable text, including notes on readings, by using a keyboard, although keyboarding may be difficult for some to learn. Alternative keyboards may be helpful, since they allow the user to customize the layout and appearance of the keys.

Spelling difficulties, a hallmark of dyslexia, can be addressed with a combination of common spell checker, word prediction software, and voice synthesizer. Word prediction can be helpful to people with keyboarding, spelling, or grammar problems or difficulty coming up with the right word.

People with memory and organizational problems, as well as those who have difficulty expressing their thoughts in writing, can be assisted with outlining and brainstorming or mind mapping programs. Information gathering and later reorganization are simplified.

Other conditions that affect learning include attention deficit disorder (ADD), attention deficit hyperactivity disorder (ADHD), autism, and mental retardation. Some of the adaptations that help people with learning disabilities are also useful to those with ADD and ADHD, especially since many of them also have LD. Carrels, small study rooms and other settings with minimum distraction are helpful to both groups, but essential to many with ADD or ADHD. Headphones block out extraneous noise and also reduce the general sound level in the library.

Figure 1.1 gives an overview of the possibilities of adaptive technology for aiding persons with disabilities. The following chapters will describe how to make Websites accessible and how to discern which ones are not accessible, plus how to adapt your computers, budgets, and staff to facilitate access for all.

	VISUALLY IMPAIRED	BLIND	LEARNING DISABLED	DEAF	HEARING IMPAIRED	NON-DISABLED	PHYSICALLY HANDICAPPED
LARGE MONITOR	•		•			•	•
ANTIGLARE FILTER	•		•			•	•
TEXT ENLARGING SOFTWARE	•		•				
COLOR / BRIGHTNESS KEY	•		•			•	
LARGE-PRINT KEYTOPS	•		•			•	
LARGE-PRINT OUTPUT	•		•				
BRAILLE KEYTOPS		•					
RAISED-DOT HOME KEYS	•		•			•	
SCREEN READER / SYNTHESIZER	•	•	•				
BRAILLE SOFTWARE TRANSLATOR		•					
REFRESHABLE BRAILLE DISPLAY		•					
BRAILLE PRINTER		•					
SPEECH RECOGNITION	•	•	•				•
SHOW SOUNDS			•	•	•		
CAPTIONING TEXT			•	•	•		
ALTERNATE KEYBOARDS							•
TRACKBALLS							•
SCREEN DISPLAY KEYBOARDS							•
KEY GUARD							•
TEXT BROWSER SOFTWARE	•	•					
HEADPHONES			•		•		
OCR SCANNING	•	•	•				
TEXT EXPLAINING VISUAL	•	•	•				

FIGURE 1.1
Varied accessibility solutions

Notes

1. The National Library Service (NLS) for the Blind and Physically Handicapped is a division of the Library of Congress and works with a network of cooperating agencies throughout the United States (and territories) to deliver leisure-reading materials to qualified U.S. citizens. More information can be found at <lcweb.loc.gov/nls>. Recordings for the Blind and Dyslexic (RB&D) is an independent organization whose mission is to provide print impaired persons with textbook materials that help them reach educational goals. More information can be found at <www.rfbd.org>.
2. Barbara Hoffert, "Book Report: What Public Libraries Buy and How Much They Spend," *Library Journal* 123, no. 3 (February 15, 1998): 106.
3. Larry Goldberg, "Electronic Curb Cuts: Equitable Access to the Future," Boston: WGBH. Available at <www.wgbh.org>.
4. Bill Gates, "Helping People with Disabilities Helps Everybody," *New York Times,* August 13, 1997.
5. Reuters Ltd., "Making the Internet More Accessible to Blind, Disabled," CNN Interactive, October 22, 1997.
6. Eric Bergman and Earl Johnson, "Towards Accessible Human-Computer Interaction," excerpted from *Advances in Human-Computer Interaction,* ed. Jakob Nielson, vol. 5 (Norwood, N.J.: Ablex, 1995).

2

Click (W)Here(?)!—Basic Document Design

Because medical research concludes that each human being has a unique genetic code, a standard prescription for "adaptive Internet access" cannot be written. Instead, tools such as screen readers, refreshable Braille displays, and text enlargers may be purchased and offered to patrons with disabilities so they themselves will choose and use what will help them. One item that can be standardized, however, and will help all people with or without disabilities, is a commitment to good Web design.

One authoritative source to consult for guidelines regarding accessible HyperText Markup Language (HTML) tagging is the World Wide Web Consortium (W3C), which on April 7, 1997, announced the launch of its Web Accessibility Initiative (WAI) to promote and achieve Web functionality for people with disabilities. Tim Berners-Lee, director of the W3C and inventor of the WWW, said, "The W3C is committed to removing accessibility barriers for all people with disabilities, including the deaf, blind, physically challenged, and cognitive or visually impaired. We plan to work aggressively with government, industry, and community leaders to establish and attain Web accessibility goals."[1] Initially, the group's focus will be to develop protocols and data formats aimed at making the Web itself more accessible, but it has also completed the first "Public Working Draft of WAI Page Author Guidelines" to aid those who want to use accessible tagging in their HTML documents.[2] To meet the accessibility goals of the W3C, the Websites and resource pages must be accessible to all patrons. It is very helpful to be aware of Web design principles advocated by organizations that specialize in accessible design. These organizations include Disabilities, Opportunities, Internetworking, and Technology (DO-IT) (<www.weber.u.washington.edu/~doit>), Starling Access Services (<www.starlingweb.com>), and the Trace Center at the University of Wisconsin-Madison (<www.trace.wisc.edu>). These organizations advocate adherence to universal design principles to transcend the limitations of HTML documents.

Universal Design Principles for Web Pages

The Trace Center's definition of universal design is "the process of creating products (devices, environments, systems, and processes) that are usable by people with the widest range of abilities, operating within the widest possible range of situations (environments, conditions, and circumstances).[3]

DO-IT also advocates universal design principles to guarantee access for those who

cannot see graphics because of visual impairments.

cannot hear audio because of hearing impairments.

use slow connections and modems or older equipment that cannot download large files.

have difficulty navigating sites that are poorly organized with unclear directions because they have learning disabilities, speak English as a second language, or are younger than the average user.

use adaptive technology with their computer to access the Web (<www.weber.u.washington.edu/~doit/Brochures/Technology/universal.design.html>).

The Web page designer addressing universal design and accessibility is more concerned with information dissemination for all, rather than visual appeal for most. When designing the document, an attempt is made to make all the material displayed as accessible as possible, whether it is a menu item, graphic, or video clip. Creating accessible Web pages may not take additional money, just more time and consideration.

HTML for Adaptive Technology

HTML is the markup method used for documents or pages found on the World Wide Web. The site's designer can use this code to create hypertext references to other HTML pages and resources, both within the site or anywhere else on the Internet. HTML code uses American Standard Code for Information Interchange (ASCII) text and can be created using text editors. Web documents are coded or marked up with tags that will tell the program where the author wants pages to end, when he or she wants a list created, when he or she wants a statement emphasized.

Using HTML correctly will enable screen readers and refreshable Braille display to interpret the information on the site as the page's author wishes it to be seen. It is not difficult, once you begin to think in a text mode rather than a visual or artistic mode. Using HTML correctly will present the site for the user using adaptive technology. Screen readers, for example, always start reading left to right and always at the same pitch, while people using their natural vision will probably start reading in a variety of places before settling in on the first sentence.

Avoid underlining text, as partially sighted individuals will have a hard time discerning the actual text with the line grazing the bottom of the letters. It is also wise to avoid capitalizing whole words, for persons with low vision or with a learning disability may have a difficult time discerning the beginning and the end of a word.

It is always advisable to test the pages on the mainstream browsers such as Netscape and Internet Explorer as well as Lynx, to make sure alternative text is viewable and complete. Also, send the pages to an online accessibility clearing site such as Bobby, created by the Center for Applied Special Technology (CAST), which will highlight nonstandard and incorrect HTML used, as well as a myriad of other features.

Solid-Color Backgrounds

The background chosen for Websites and home pages is important to those using adaptive devices to access information. A solid color is always a good choice and patterns or textures should be avoided. For instance, graceful morning glories used as a background for a directory menu may be visually appealing for users without print disabilities, but impossible for a person with low vision or a learning disability to read. A better choice would be to make the background solid blue and the print white. While it is advisable to use one of the 16 colors that a 16-color Video Graphics Array (VGA) adapter can support, the color chosen is not so important as the contrast between the background and text.

Test the background on a black-and-white monitor as well as on several sizes and qualities of color monitors. Black and white will help you decide if the color contrast is sufficient. Some colors do not translate to black and white well (many users of screen readers set their monitors on black and white), nor hold their color resolution on oversize monitors. Larger monitors do not always have the ability to absorb all of the pixels involved in creating shades of tertiary colors.

Consistent Page Layout and Length

Consistency is very important for users of your site. Important features of your page design should be in the same place on every page of your site. Knowing where directional buttons, messages, and menus are located will allow users to find what they need quickly and efficiently. While creativity may tempt you to tinker with your page design, don't—make it right and then leave it alone.

It is helpful, when producing long documents, to include a Table of Contents with links to key sections and the ability to return to the home page and Table of Contents at will. This is necessary for users of screen readers who may wish to use the Review command of their screen reader to skim the article before actually reading it.

Clear Links

Most users of the World Wide Web will admit that links to external sites are the most intriguing and enjoyable part of the surfing experience, for you don't know exactly where you will end up. So care should be taken to ensure that all the links you add can be easily found. If possible, try to avoid using the term "Click here," for it may not be obvious to everyone where "here" is. The required action should be evident, as Internet users already know that you need to "click" to travel onward.

Avoid multiple links in one sentence or paragraph. For instance, this sentence will not be clearly understood by a screen reader: "We are a *Frescia County* Agency serving *families in transition.* Our goal is to locate *low-cost housing* for the *homeless of Frescia County* by *job retraining* and by teaching *household budgeting* and *parenting skills.* We also maintain an *Information and Referral Directory* at *Frescia County Main Library."*

While the developers of the site want to convey that they are a Frescia County Agency whose mission is to find housing for homeless families, and the site offers links to further information on household budgeting, parenting skills, and job retraining programs, the screen reader may miss the hypertext links. It would be preferable to offer an introductory paragraph stating the mission of the agency and then offer links in a single column.

Likewise, links should be written in a manner that is not distracting to the user. For instance, a sun that smiles and scrolls the command to "Click here for hours and events" is not so understandable as a steady sun smile button with a text description of the smiling sun stating "hours and events." Persons with learning disabilities may be distracted by the blinking sun and persons with low vision may not be able to follow the scrolling bar.

It is wise to avoid using images without descriptive text as links. While most users may think that "Click here for more" under the picture of a book will bring up a similar list of books, persons with learning disabilities may not interpret it as such, and people using screen readers will not know what it is. It may be better to write (using brackets): "[Click here for similar titles on subject]" or even better "[More titles of the subject]." If you use a graphic, be sure to include supplementary text.

If you use icons to represent hypertext links, be sure the chosen icon is large enough for someone with mobility impairment to "find the target" for the click.

Single Columns When Possible

Generally speaking, avoid the use of tables to create multiple columns, if possible. Remember that screen readers read left to right, which means a three-column directory document will be misread by the reader. The director of Starling Access Services suggests using headings, paragraphs, lists, and definition elements creatively to present information in a more accessible manner. It is helpful to end items on the lists or sentences with appropriate punctuation marks, for the screen readers do recognize and translate them for the user.

If you definitely want to use tables to create columns, you will have to experiment with modifications to table markup for the content in the columns to be rendered in the correct order by a text browser or screen reader. For example, placing a <BR> tag at the end of a row in a table will create a break in text that a browser or reader will recognize as a signal to move on to the next line of text.

Screen reader developers are currently working on methods to have their software read within a table rather than across columns.

Alternate Text Graphics

Yes, you are proud of your new building and you are correct in wanting it displayed on your Website. When you incorporate the graphic, however, you need to offer a succinct description for the visually impaired visitor. Duplicating the text in the <ALT TEXT> element of the <IMG SRC> tag will allow users with screen readers to read the description you formulate. Using the <ALT TEXT> tag allows nonsighted users to read descriptions without forcing sighted users to view them. The National Center for Accessible Media (NCAM) also suggests using a "D" link to take the user who needs more description to another page where the author of the page has space to fully describe the image.

It is also wise to avoid placing more than one photograph on a page for the resulting <ALT TEXT> may be incorrectly interpreted by the screen unless you are sure you are using a good design reader. For instance, a Website home page welcoming visitors to visit Cleveland for its myriad of activities may show a picture of the mayor, the new Louis Stokes wing of the Cleveland Public Library, the Rock and Roll Hall of Fame, and Jacob's Field. The screen reader reading only the <ALT TEXT> tags may interpret the page as "The Mayor of Cleveland, Louis Stokes Wing, Rock and Roll, Jacob's Field" or may only pick up the words "Mayor, Wing, Roll, Jacob's Field," which really says nothing about anything.

When graphics are used as image maps, which allow different areas of the image to represent hypertext links to other documents, it is important to provide alternate means of selecting items directly above or below the image map. Instructions for the user who is relying on a screen reader should also be included.[4]

Frames

Using frames can create a page that is inaccessible to those using screen readers. If frames are necessary, an effective alternative to the frames page should be included. The <NOFRAME> tag should always be included when using framed pages. This tag allows entire documents to be displayed in browsers that are incapable of displaying frames.

Lists with Bullets and Numbers

Very often when quickly skimming Websites our eyes will be drawn to lists, for we know that lists offer a summation of the text and the bullets or numbers indicate what the author wants us to read. With screen readers, however, bullets may be interpreted as dots, asterisks, or periods. Instead of using text bullets in an HTML document, use the correct tagging: <UL> to start the bulleted list; <LI> before each bulleted item; and </UL> to end the list. Browsers will interpret these tags and insert correctly formatted bullets before each item. Always remember to add a period at the end of each item on the list. This will tell the screen reader that it is at the end of one item and will allow it to move on to the next item on the list.

Similarly, numbered lists should not be created by inserting numbers in the HTML text document, but rather by using appropriate tagging: <OL> to start the numbered list, <LI> before each numbered item, and </OL> to end the list.

Online Forms

Forms are yet another roadblock for screen readers, although screen-reading developers are confident that they will find a solution to the problems encountered, according to Judith Dixon in an article in *Library Hi Tech*.[5] Readers do not know where the fill-in box is, how many lines must be filled out, or when they have reached the end of the form. Thus, if you wish visitors to your site to fill out electronic applications, offer an alternative method, such as a simple "mail to" link that could ask them to submit the same information in e-mail messages.

Other options would be to offer the ability to download the form as a text or PDF file, or to put up an image that could be printed out. The user would then have a paper version of the form that could be filled out and submitted.

Captioning Sound

Many Websites now include audio clips as part of their information presentation. Appropriately used audio clips, such as a reading of Langston

Hughes' poetry on a special-events page announcing a poetry day at the community center, make the site enjoyable, educational, and informational. While computer users who are visually impaired or learning disabled would actually benefit from this oral feature, users who are deaf or hard of hearing would miss the creativity that went into formulating this page unless the site was linked to a captioned version or a transcription of the reading. A text translation would allow the user who is deaf to "hear" the poetry.

Add Menus to Maps

Adding a location map to your Website is useful for patrons who can see and interpret it, but for persons without vision (screen browsers do not interpret images such as maps and may take the user down a circular pathway) or persons with conceptual disabilities, maps are useless. Including an alternative menu of the information on the image will ensure that all patrons find your information.

Text Descriptions for Java Applets

Simply stated, all HTML Java Applet tags should contain a short text description. This is valuable to users who are using screen readers (also for those not having a Java-capable browser).

Validating Your Pages

When you finally complete your Web page, send it to Bobby, a Web-based validation service developed and maintained by CAST.[6] This Web-based service will help ensure that you have followed all the rules that allow access to people with disabilities. All that you need to do once you are interfaced with Bobby (and have read the updated instructions) is to enter the Universal Resource Locator (URL) of the site you want checked and submit the information. Bobby will then analyze the tagging in your document and display an annotated version of the original page. Whenever an access problem is perceived, a picture of Bobby's hat with the disability access symbol will appear.

Clicking on the hat itself will bring an explanation of the perceived access problem. The Bobby program is so sophisticated that it can also discern if browser compatibility problems exist. In the case of such problems, a plain hat will appear.

Again, clicking on the hat will tell you the problem. Bobby will also offer you possible solutions. Bobby checks for many items.

BOBBY PATROLS ACCESSIBILITY AND LOOKS FOR:

1. Missing alternative text descriptions for images.
2. Missing alternative text descriptions for image maps.
3. Inaccessible links or links that probably will not be found by a screen reader. These links may be in places such as sidebars or pull-down menus. These may also be difficult for users with mobility impairment to use.
4. Problems with HTML table tagging.
5. BLINK and MARQUEE tags that cannot be read by screen readers and are distracting to users with learning disabilities.
6. Too many words in an alternative text description. Bobby says 20 words is the maximum number needed. If you feel 20 words isn't enough, Bobby suggests a D link.
7. Adjacent links that aren't separated. Browsers need words or breaks between links or the links will run together.
8. Confusing links such as the infamous "Click here" or "Click this" will be noted, for they are nondescriptive. Bobby always advises that descriptive text be used.
9. Text links with more than ten words will be highlighted as bad design. Too many words in a hypertext link will cause the link to wrap across multiple lines.
10. Background colors or images with conflicts of text to background and distraction of backgrounds in general. Background images may cause the text to dissolve or present distraction to users who cannot filter the information.
11. Smileys—:)—are frowned on by Bobby's developers. They say "we hate to be grinches, but try to avoid using smileys on your Web pages for screen readers for the blind and learning disabled will read smileys literally, i.e., "colon, close parenthesis."
12. Tables without texts. If Bobby finds an HTML table without a text description, it will suggest the addition of a text-only link.
13. HTML forms that do not have keyboard input will be pointed out. People with limited dexterity will not be able to move the cursor to the lines that need to be filled in and users who are blind will not see the boxes that they need to fill in.
14. Audio files that do not have descriptive text. While audio files help those who are blind, they add challenges to those who are deaf or hard of hearing. Bobby suggests you always include use captioning.
15. Frames without alternative texts. A frame-based page should always include an alternative layout, such as the <No Frame> option.

Bobby will also check your site to see how various browsers will interact with it by checking the accuracy of the tagging in your document. It will point out tags that it does not recognize, for this means that browsers will not recognize them either. It looks for misplaced tags in tables and forms, and makes sure that all tags have a properly placed opening and closing tag so that browsers will interpret the entire document correctly.

After Bobby checks your page, pointing out problems and offering suggestions, it will summarize the accessibility errors in what Bobby's developers feel are the order of importance. The errors closest to the top of the report are the most important to change. Because the items are ranked, Bobby is able to compute the accessibility score for the page, giving it a ranking of one, two, three, or four stars. A four-star page entitles the page to use the "Bobby approved icon" (see figure 2-1).

If you feel that you have followed accessibility guidelines in the creation of your Web pages and have passed Bobby's validation process, you might want to announce to your users that yours is an accessible site. In cooperation with the Trace Center and other professionals in the area of assistive technology, the CPB/WGBH NCAM provides the Web Access Symbol, which can be used by authors of Web pages to denote that their sites contain accessibility features that will accommodate the needs of disabled users. The symbol and its accompanying <ALT TEXT> description ["Web Access Symbol (for people with disabilities)"] can be downloaded from the NCSM Web pages at <www.wgbh.org/wgbh/pages/ncam/symbolwinner.html> (see figure 2-2).

But What Makes a Website Great?

Kathy Gill, Website author of *eNetDigest,* succinctly answers the question of what makes a great Website in one word—content.[7] She goes on to say that there is a place for Shockwave, Java, Real Audio, and whatever is yet to come, but content should come first and foremost in site development and maintenance. She also maintains that a site should have maximum

FIGURE 2-1
Bobby approved icon

FIGURE 2-2
Web Access Symbol

browser compatibility and recommends working with Lynx (a text-based browser) because if Lynx can view a document, Braille displays and screen browsers should be able to interpret it correctly as well.

Also remember that at times we all experience some type of "virtual" disability in our cyperspace explorations. We may be "virtually hearing impaired" because we are trying to work in a noisy environment where we can't hear spoken computer commands or signals, or we may be "virtually color blind" because we're stuck using older monitors without the latest SVGA components. Rick Cook, in his article entitled "Best Practices: Web Design for Everyone Including the Disabled," astutely pointed out that having Websites validated by a source such as Bobby is in reality a "sanity check for Web designers," as it reminds designers to be "consistent and simple, and not cute for cute's sake."[8] Web designers should also test their sites with a variety of browser software, different versions of that software, and on different computer platforms.

If you adhere to the WC3's Accessibility Guidelines, you will have the most accessible Website possible. It will be one that all persons with or without disabilities will be able to use. Even if you do not qualify for Bobby's four-star rating, you and your Website patrons will know you made the attempt and at the very least will probably be able to read more of what you were offering than if you made no attempt at all.

Notes

1. World Wide Web Consortium, "World Wide Web Consortium (W3C) Launches International Web Accessibility Initiative, W3C Leads Program to Make the Web Accessible for People with Disabilities," press release, May 6, 1997, p. 1.
2. Version 8 of the HTML Page Author checklist is available at <www.w3.org/WAI/>.
3. The Trace Center, University of Wisconsin-Madison, "Designing a More Usable World," 3; available at <www.trace.wisc.edu/publications/3.html>.
4. Judith Dixon, "Leveling the Road Ahead," *Library Hi Tech* 53, 14:1 (1996): 67.
5. Ibid.
6. Bobby was created at the Center for Applied Special Technology (CAST). Founded in 1984, CAST is a nonprofit organization whose mission is to expand opportunity for all people—especially those with disabilities—through the innovative uses of computer technology. CAST's funding comes from a variety of sources, including individuals, corporations, and government grants. It is available at <www.cast.org/bobby>.
7. Kathy Gill, "What Makes a Great Web Site?" eNetDigest, Review Criteria (September 1997); available at <www.enetdigest.com/design/review.html>.
8. Rick Cook, "Best Practices: Web Design for Everyone Including the Disabled," Netscape Enterprise Developer (August 1996); available at <www.netscapeworld.com/netscapeworld/nw-08-1996/nw-08-bestpract.html>.

3

Large-Print Access to the Internet

Perhaps the adaptive technology that can be added which will get the most use is large-print access to the computers and subsequently to the Internet. Large print stands to aid several groups of people with disabilities: those whose vision is diminishing and those with learning disabilities who have difficulty processing standard-print information.

People with visual impairments, but with sufficient vision to see letters, may prefer to access materials found online by sight. They may also use a speech synthesizer if the text is lengthy and much research is necessary.

Some people with learning disabilities often benefit from large-print displays. Enlarged letters displayed on a contrasting background allow the user to interpret letters and form words with less difficulty.

Two components are needed to yield good screen magnification and access to information: screen-enlargement software and hardware suitable for handling the display.

Software Products

Screen-magnification software enables people with sensory impairments to enlarge the screen display by virtually any factor they choose. The programs run simultaneously with the operating system and applications and can be programmed to enlarge certain areas of the screen or the entire display.

Screen Magnification in Mainstream Utilities

A few mainstream browsers and word processors allow the user to enlarge the display, and Microsoft's Windows 95 has accessibility features built into its operating system. These are products that are probably owned and used on a fairly regular basis. Their products will provide learning disabled users with the maximum enlargement possible.

Netscape 3 (Or Higher)

Netscape is a popular browser and contains utilities that allow the user to specify the size of the font displayed, as well as the colors of the display. While the options are easy to change, help will probably be required to make the needed changes, for the initial display will be in standard print and in boxes. The steps to increase the font size are easy to follow. Simply:

1. Go to the Options menu.
2. Choose General Preferences.
3. Choose Fonts.
4. There are two Choose Size buttons.
   a. One will select the proportionally spaced type.
   b. One will select the fixed width of the font.
5. Select the sizes required.
6. Choose OK.

All changes will be reflected on most Websites that are visited and Internet connections that are made. (Some Web designers override font selection with their own font definitions, which can adversely affect the browser settings.)

If your only accessibility option is to use Netscape's accessibility features, it will be necessary to allow users to adapt the browser with each search. Be sure that the display monitor is oversize (19 inches or larger).

Netscape also allows the users to adjust all the colors of the screen display. This includes foreground, background, text display, and links. To adjust all these items does take a little work, but could help the user.

1. Go to the Options menu.
2. Choose General Preferences.
3. Choose Colors.
4. Under Color Control, choose Use My Colors For.
   a. Choose colors needed for links, followed links, and text to appear in.
   b. Under Background, select Custom and choose the color needed.
5. Review and make any changes.
6. Choose OK.

Microsoft Internet Explorer, Explorer NT, Word, Works, and Encarta

Microsoft's Internet Explorer (versions 3.1 and higher) as well as its other mass-market software products allow the user to change the size of the text for viewing on-screen and have it carried forward in the printed document. While the magnification included will not be large enough for the most severely visually impaired, it will aid those patrons who are starting to lose vision and those patrons who can comprehend words more easily when they are displayed in large, bold type. While all the fonts can be made to display and print in bold or a point size larger than 14 point, most would not be usable by persons with visual and comprehension disabilities. The fonts believed to be most accessible are Arial, Century Gothic, Tahoma, Tahoma Bold, and Verdana, for they do not have serifs and are not script or calligraphy.

Changing the size of the text displays in Internet Explorer are simply explained by Microsoft as "Click on the View menu, point to Fonts, then click the size you want." The instructions for Encarta are similar, for they instruct the user "to increase text size, click on the Options menu, point to Text Size, then click the text size you want." The problem with these instructions and the actual procedures is that a person with low vision will have difficulty seeing the instructions and viewing the displays because all the information is written in standard print so the user will need help until the display is adjusted. If the user wants to do anything more than browse the Web, just changing the text size is not sufficient; screen-enlargement software will be necessary.

The Microsoft products (Windows 95 or later) also contain a few other features geared toward accessibility. The products allow the use of high-contrast settings to view the displays. The instructions given to activate the utility are:

1. After starting the programs, click on Settings; then click on the Control Panel.
2. Click on Accessibility Options; then on the File menu, click Open.
3. Click the Display tab; then click Use High Contrast.
4. The displays automatically available will be White on Black or Black on White; choose one or customize one.

Two other features worth noting that can be accessed through the Control Panel line are the abilities to enlarge the size of the mouse pointer, change its color, and slow it down, and invoke the Sounds option that will auditorily announce items such as the opening and closing of programs or minimizing or maximizing the size of windows.

A review of the product by the *Journal of Visual Impairment and Blindness* News Service noted that Microsoft has two products that it sells separately, IntelliType (keyboard software) and IntelliPoint (mouse software, available with the newest model of the Microsoft mouse), which are useful for persons with low vision.[1] With both products, the mouse pointer can be located using a sonar function. When the control key is pressed, a shrinking circle appears around the mouse pointer, highlighting its location. Both can automatically place the mouse pointer over the default button when a dialogue box is opened. In IntelliPoint, it is possible to activate a "cometlike trail" for the mouse pointer and slow down the speed of its movement over icons, buttons, and other controls. For further information on the accessibility features of Microsoft's products, visit Microsoft's Website, for printed information is sparse.[2]

Separate Screen-Magnification Programs

Screen-magnification programs allow the user with low vision to access computer information by enlarging the display on the screen by any factor he or she needs. These products, which are usually included in the higher-end magnification programs, offer a wide range of magnification options to the users and allow them to tailor the display to accommodate their particular type of disability. Some products will allow the user to enlarge the text and shrink the screen, to provide one-line-at-a-time access. Some programs enlarge the entire screen, while others only enlarge the area around the mouse, producing a moving enlargement area. Other programs provide a set of mouse-tracking features such as the option to link the mouse pointer to the screen movement and limit the movement to horizontal or vertical directions only. These features are extremely helpful when using the Internet.

Additionally, screen-magnification programs offer the user a variety of screen options for viewing the magnified area of the screen. A user can use the software to split the screen into magnified and unmagnified areas and to move across the page at a preset speed (usually as fast as the user's vision permits him or her to read).

This is the ideal solution to address the needs of visually impaired users, for problems with compatibility usually lie with resident video drivers such as those installed in Microsoft's products. Many manufacturers recommend installing their products on a specific driver and give advised resolution and color-depth settings. Research specialists admit that installing the programs is tricky, although some developers have been working directly with the major market products to resolve incompatibility issues. Always check with the manufacturer before purchasing to ensure that the software is compatible with the video card that is installed. Following are several discussions of popular screen-magnification software programs.

ZoomText for Windows and ZoomText Xtra Level II

The ZoomText family of software products was developed by the Ai Squared Corporation. The Zoom windows can be customized to the user's preference by using full- or partial-screen window types and displaying up to six windows at once. There are 11 magnification levels and "edge smoothing" to eliminate distortions caused by enlarging standardized text. The user can scroll to view any portion of the split screen in a Zoom window. The Review mode allows the user to automatically jump to a targeted area of the screen by using a hotkey. Another feature of ZoomText is that it allows the user to keep track of screen activity such as text entry, mouse movement, and the selection of menus and controls. Ai Squared offers a free demonstration diskette of its product.[3]

ZoomText Xtra Level II (see figure 3-1) incorporates all the previously mentioned features, but adds a huge plus—synthesized screen-reading capabilities, which will read windows and text. It is compatible with Windows 95, 98, and NT.

Why is this important? First, it helps those users who prefer screen magnification, but who occasionally need the assistance of screen readers. Before this product was developed, a separate screen reader and a screen magnifier needed to be purchased and installed so that they would work both independently and in conjunction with each other. Secondly, a workstation can be developed that is accessible by users who are visually impaired and prefer print but need speech output as well, users who are learning disabled and need speech output, and users who are blind and need speech output. There will be instances where the user who is blind may encounter difficulty.

When the product was reviewed by the University of Toronto, reviewers found that while problems did occur, the product will work with browsers such as Netscape and Internet Explorer, and that the quality of the screen reader was acceptable. It was recommended that the user purchase the fastest computer available with at least 64 MB RAM to incorporate all the features and still be able to access the Internet.[4]

ZoomText is trying to develop a solution for access to Windows NT, as well as working on Level 3 of ZoomText Xtra, which will add scanning, Optical Character Recognition (OCR), form filling, and printing to the product line. Ai Squared also hopes to develop a software program for people with learning disabilities as well.

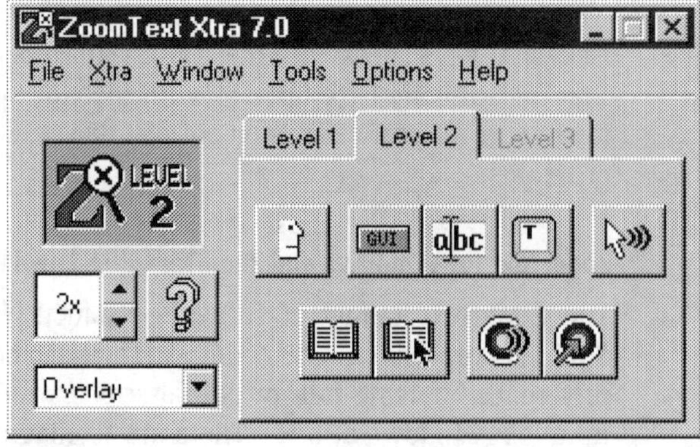

FIGURE 3-1
ZoomText Xtra screen

LP-Windows

LP-Windows is a product of Visionware that allows the user to use a menu system to magnify and stretch text on monitors. Visionware offers prospective purchasers a free 20-minute demonstration diskette.[5]

LP-Windows' program menu, which allows the user to make a myriad of changes to the display, is activated by pressing the <LEFT-SHIFT> twice. At that point the user is asked to choose the font size he or she wishes. The patron can use the menu to select the magnification needed. It is activated when <MAGNIFY> is clicked. The Magnify and Stretch box appears as well as a key sequence on the numeric pad of the keyboard. Keying in the initial font display creates a menu that is easier to use.

While there are commands that allow the user to use hotkeys to make all the display changes, everything can be accomplished through the menu. One can also choose to split the screen (the advantage is the user has a better interpretation of the total presentation), enlarge the mouse pointer, or change the way to navigate the mouse on the magnified display, use an infinite amount of color combinations for presentation, track the text, and pan the document.

Evaluated by resource specialists, LP-Windows was found to have the ability to smooth the "stretched fonts" and pan documents at a prescribed speed and distance. The product worked well with Netscape and all Internet browsers. The product also worked well with an independently installed speech program.[6]

Panorama Windows Bridge

Panorama, a product of Syntha-Voice Computers, a Canadian company headquartered in Ontario with U.S. offices in Niagara Falls, New York, is popular with North American users. The product allows the user to feel at home within the graphical environment of Microsoft's Windows by using the same access commands for navigation (a plus for staff and patrons alike).

Panorama Windows products will allow the user to adjust font size, color displays, and scrolling ability by word, line, or paragraph. An added feature is that the Large-Print Window automatically adjusts to focus on messages or prompts that may appear outside the viewing window.

Additionally, Windows Bridge, a screen reader, allows the user to control the navigation of the mouse pointer from the keyboard, if desired. A big plus is that Panorama contains a Mouse Search command that will allow the user to instantly move the mouse pointer to a specific location such as an icon or menu selection.

The product also includes a Icon Label Library, which contains descriptive labels for more than 1,000 commonly used Windows icons, as well as a feature that allows the user to point at any icon on the screen and instantly receive a descriptive label for the image.

Syntha-Voice provides potential purchasers with a demonstration of its product. Syntha-Voice also offers an audiocassette tutorial and maintains an online tutorial and manual.

Hardware Approach—Vista PCI and Super Vista

Vista PCI and Super Vista for Windows are part of a family of screen-enlarging hardware developed by Telesensory Corporation. Features of the hardware, in addition to a wide array of magnification, include magnifying the portion of the screen being viewed while displaying the rest in its standard presentation.

One unique feature offered by Vista includes the ability to locate the user's place within the environment with a "ruler line" of magnification that moves around the screen when directed. The Vista family also comes with a plug-in printed circuit board and a large three-button mouse that is used to control the system.

Vista PCI is the product of many years of work by Telesensory, which realized it needed to develop a product that would work with software systems currently used by public and academic libraries. The company sought out the major vendors and attempted to develop a product that will work in harmony with networks, terminal emulation systems, and workstations to online public access catalogs (OPACs) and other online resource materials provided by libraries. The product of these labors is Vista PCI, which provides direct screen magnification of all the text and graphics and is adjusted by using a three-button mouse or keypad. The product allows the user to make the standard adjustments to the display, such as increase the size of the display font, change the colors of the display, use an electronic magnified ruler, and have dual screens as well as the ability to magnify certain areas of the screen. While Vista PCI does not have all the attributes of specialized screen magnifiers, it is the only hardware product which was developed in harmony with many of the library automation systems. A big plus of Vista PCI is that, with a companion product, V Voice, it can be used to create a workstation that can be employed by persons with visual impairment, blindness, or learning disabilities.

Telesensory provides the user manual on diskette and a demonstration diskette on request. In addition to providing product information at its Website, Telesensory maintains an excellent Website whose format can serve as a model in design and accessibility.[7]

Hardware for Large-Print Displays

A key piece of hardware for large-print displays is an oversize monitor. Although standard monitors (14 inches) are used by many persons using screen-enlargement software, they do not allow the user to fully take advantage of screen enhancement. Larger display monitors (19 to 20 inches) allow more of the text to be viewed. Flat displays are preferred because they reduce distortion on large screens. Oversize monitors are available commercially from mainstream vendors, as well as those specializing in adapted technology.

Low-Vision Reading Systems

Several hardware solutions are available to broaden access to printed and displayed text. Following are devices that will increase the size of text, diagrams, and illustrations to an easier-to-view size.

Clearview VGA

Clearview VGA reading system is manufactured by HumanWare and provides the user with enlarged access to materials found via the computer, as well as those materials found in print. This is facilitated by adding a movable reading table that is part of a Closed-Circuit Television (CCTV) system.

While these modifications are not so varied as those of specialized software products, the user is able to choose 14 different color combinations for the display, split the screen, and choose font magnification on a line-by-line basis.

In addition to the simplistic magnification, this product will work with the software programs listed previously. HumanWare will provide a no-obligation demonstration at a library facility to determine product compatibility.[8]

Optelec Spectrum SVGA

The Optelec Spectrum system is compatible with most systems and allows the user access to any printed materials (including handwritten documents), as well as access to text and graphics found online. This is possible because of the addition of a CCTV (see figure 3-2). The CCTV will enlarge newspaper print from half an inch to more than four inches, allowing the user to read newspapers not found online. With the CCTV feature, the user with low vision can read personal mail and replay unassisted. The display is clear and the display's foreground and background can be manipulated.

If budgeting is an issue, this product, along with activating the accessibilities features of products such as Netscape or Microsoft's Explorer, will serve to help many low-vision patrons. It may not be the final solution, but it is a good starting point.

Optelec will provide a no-obligation demonstration at your site or advise you of facilities using the product.[9]

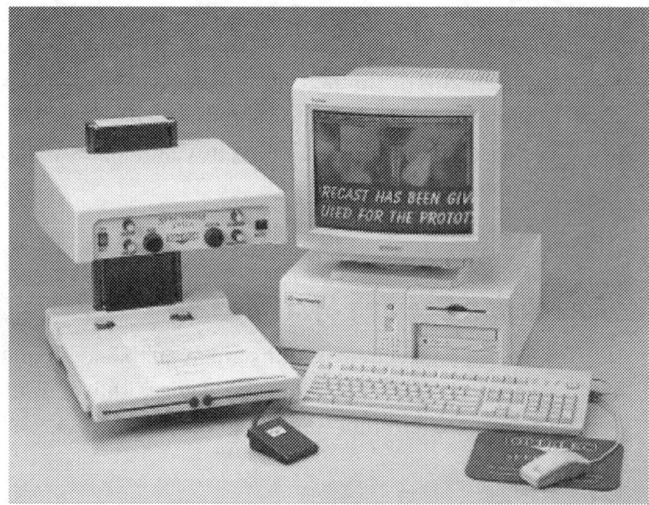

FIGURE 3-2
Optelec Spectrum system with CCTV

Other Aids to Large-Print Access

Additional factors must be considered when accessing large-print facilities.

Large-Print Keytops

These are for the people who never learned to type without looking at their fingers and the keys. Large print makes it easier for patrons with low vision or patrons with learning disabilities to "see" the keys. The letters and symbols of the large-print keytops fill the entire key surface (see figure 3-3), while in the standard display, the letters are relegated to the top left third of the key surface.

These press-ply keytop labels are available in high-contrast displays, are economical, and easy to install. They do hold up with public usage. They can be viewed on the Hooleon Website.[10]

FIGURE 3-3
Actual size of large-print keytop display

Good Lighting

Good lighting in the area where the large-print workstation is situated is as essential as providing the hardware and the software needed. A good task lamp or magnifying task lamp placed in the workstation will allow the patron with low vision to find and read large-print instructions as well see the keyboard and other items needed to feel comfortable in the work area.

Magnifying task lamps are available through vendors of specialized adaptive products as well as vendors selling craft equipment. While a halogen lamp provides the maximum amount of light, there have been reports of the lamps overheating, so it is best to use an incandescent light or a fluorescent Ott Light. The latter provides the user with a semblance of natural light and can be found at craft and hobby stores. Many people with visual impairments are sensitive to light, however, so eliminating glare in work areas should be considered.

Easy Access to Workstation and Clear Signage

Well-meaning intentions often put large-print workstations in areas of the library where the user can enjoy maximum privacy. This means that the low-vision patron must take a path filled with the unintentional obstacles of step stools, book trucks, and crawling children. Try to locate the accessible workstation with the other workstations or as close to the service desk as possible. In facilities where this is not feasible, remind staff to keep library materials out of potential pathways and remind parents and patrons that children may be afoot.

Also avoid using signage that has serifs. Simple block lettering is easiest to discern by both patrons with low vision and by those patrons with learning disabilities that cause problems interpreting letters.

Printer Capabilities for Output

Many large-print programs yield large-print output. Items found on the Internet, however, may not be formulated as such and a printer solution may need to be found. With the variety of fonts available in the standard laser jet and ink jet printer library, it is not necessary to purchase extralarge print cartridges. It is important to choose a default large-print typeface that is as easy to read in large print as it is in standard print. The chart in figure 3-4 offers a comparison of 14-point fonts (an illusion exists that they are not equal in point size).

As stated previously, choose a bold typeface without serifs or italics; people shouldn't have to figure if the letter is an *m* or an *n* or an *r*.

Also, the type produced by a dot matrix printer should not be stretched. Stretching the letters creates white spaces between the dots, making it extremely difficult for persons with visual impairments to read.

Click Here	Arial
Click Here	Lucida Sans
Click Here	Tahoma
Click Here	Veranda
Click Here	Times New Roman
Click Here	Rockwell
Click Here	Impact
Click Here	Calisto MT
Click Here	Wide Latin
Click Here	Desdemona
Click Here	Castellar
Click Here	Algerian

FIGURE 3-4

All 14-point fonts are not created equal (selected fonts from Word 97)

Large-print access is one of the easier adaptions to make and helps people born with disabilities and those who are becoming visually impaired because of age to continue to read and access materials. Do not be surprised, however, when staff and public line up to use the oversize display, for it is simply easier on the eyes and on the brain.

Notes

1. C. L. Earl and J. D. Levanthal, "Windows 95 Access for Blind or Visually Impaired Persons: An Overview," *Journal of Visual Impairment and Blindness* (September-October 1997): 6–9.
2. Additional information on Microsoft's Accessibility features can be found at <www. microsoft.com>.
3. To receive a free demonstration diskette of ZoomText's products, write: AI Squared, P.O. Box 669, Manchester Center, VT 05255; or call (802) 362-3612; or e-mail Scott Moore at <smoore@aisquared.com>. You may also receive a download of the product from their Website at <www.aisquared.com>.
4. Karen McCall, Vision Technology Specialist, "ZoomText Xtra-Beta," evaluation (Toronto: University of Toronto: Adaptive Technology Resource Centre). The review at length may be found at <www.utoronto.ca/atrc/uiap/en/zoomtext>.
5. To obtain a free demonstration diskette of the LP-Windows program, contact the distributor: Optelec U.S., Inc., 6 Lyberty Way, Westford, MA 01886; or call (800) 828-1056 or (508) 392-0707; or visit their Website at <www.optelec.com>.
6. M. M. Usland and J. C. Su, "A Review of Two Screen Magnification Programs for Windows 95: Magnum 95 and LP-Windows," *Journal of Visual Impairment and Blindness* (September 1997): 9–12.
7. To receive information about the Vista line, contact Telesensory at: Telesensory Corporation, 520 Almanor Ave., Sunnyvale, CA 94086-3533; or visit their Website at <www.telesensory.com>.

8. Contact HumanWare at: HumanWare Inc., 245 Kind Road, Suite P, Loomis, CA 95650; or call (916) 652-7253 or (800) 722-3393; or visit their Website at <www.humanware.com>.
9. Contact Optelec at Optelec U.S. Inc., 6 Lyberty Way, Westford, MA 01886; or call (800) 828-1056 or (508) 392-0707; or visit their Website at <www.optelec.com>.
10. More information can be obtained about the keytops by writing: Hooleon Corporation, 411 South 6th Street, Building B, Cottonwood, AZ 86326; or call (520) 634-4503 or (800) 937-1337; or visit their Website at <www.hooleon.com>.

4

Hearing the Internet

Users who are blind have several options when accessing computers and the Internet. They can choose to have a sighted individual read the information for them, or use a refreshable Braille display or a screen reader interfaced with a synthetic voice output.

Users who have a learning disability that prevents them from accessing standard print generally have only two choices to access printed material that they cannot read. They may choose a sighted human reader or a synthetic voice output driven by a screen reader.

Often, both types of users choose the screen readers with voice-output options. The reason is that human readers are costly and must be scheduled, and Braille is a writing format unknown to the newly blinded, persons whose vision loss is a result of diabetes, or those with a reading disability such as dyslexia. Doug Wakefield, Adaptive Technology Specialist, presents the following overview of speech access with emphasis on accessing the Internet.

Sound Effects—When Output Is Not Always Sound

Modern computers are usually equipped with both visual- and audio-output mechanisms. The visual output, or that displayed on the system's monitor, is almost always far more important than the information gained from audio output. Audio output is the sounds generated by the computer's multimedia devices. These sounds may be beeps and blips, sound effects, or musical bridges designed to accompany some Windows event such as a program or Window opening or closing (for example, the opening of Microsoft's Windows has a harplike glissando). The sounds can also be those that are retrieved and played from the Internet; these range from prerecorded sound effects to archives of famous speeches or live broadcasts from radio networks around the world.

The ability of today's computers to produce sound often leads to confusion when the subject of computer use by a blind person arises. Because blind people cannot see the screen but can usually hear audio, and a computer has an audio card and can produce sound, does that make it usable by blind people? The answer is a resounding *No*! Audio produced by a computer system that is used to enhance its output of information can be minimally useful and should never be construed as providing access for a blind person. At present, playing sounds on a computer's speakers is very much like showing graphics on the screen. That is, the sound effect can add aesthetically to the computer's output and can serve as a way to provide extra attention-grabbing warnings and alerts, but often it provides no real data.

Some might think that while these sounds may not be helpful to persons who are blind, they may be helpful to persons with learning disabilities. Again, this is a misconception; in fact, some of the sounds can be distracting to persons with learning disabilities, for many of the sounds and readings are not placed in a way that aids these users to access information and learning.

Limitations of Voice Input

Another popular myth concerning computer access for blind or visually impaired people is that blind people need to talk to a computer. A great deal of confusion often surrounds voice synthesis versus voice recognition. Voice-recognition systems rely heavily on the user being able to see the screen. While "talking" to a computer, the user is constantly monitoring the screen where the spoken words are being displayed. If a user of voice recognition sees that the computer displays the wrong word, a correction can be made. For a blind computer user, voice recognition is slow, tedious, and inaccurate and should be used only when the user is physically incapable of typing.

What Is Access?

If audio output from a computer's multimedia devices and voice input are not really accessible, then what is? To answer this question, consider the information a person needs to operate a computer. To operate a computer, whether on or off the Internet, the user must be able to carry on a conversation or dialogue with the computer. In conventional systems, the computer asks questions, displays status reports, and relays information visually on its monitor. The user talks to the computer by typing on the keyboard.

Access to a computer for a blind person or learning disabled person means being able to carry on this conversation in a nonvisual and logical manner. In short, for both groups of people, the computer either speaks through a speech synthesizer or shows its output on a Braille display simultaneously with the text display. The blind or print disabled user listens to the output and types responses.

Good access to a computer for a person who is blind or learning disabled means being able to understand the questions asked and then making appropriate responses. Also, good access means controlling and comprehending all the information that is retrieved, whether that information is contained in a text document or on a page on the Internet. Speech output is a key element in good access.

The Basics of Speech Output

How does a speech-output system work? Each system contains two major components. First is the hardware that does the "speaking." This is called a voice synthesizer because it attempts to create human-sounding speech through synthesis. Prerecorded or digitalized speech is not used. As a consequence, even the best speech synthesizers on the market still have a definite robotic quality to their sound. The second component of any speech-output system is the software program, generally referred to as a screen reader. The screen-reading program is a highly complex application that must run behind all other applications. Its job is to monitor, and send to the speech synthesizer, everything going to the computer's screen, whether from the keyboard, internal computer processing messaging and calculations, or coming into the computer from a modem or network connection (see figure 4-1).

Screen Readers—Doing It the Users' Way

A modern screen reader does more than simply monitor and repeat data. Today's screen readers provide the user with a multitude of options about how the information from the computer is to be spoken. For example, when the computer's keys are pressed, the user can choose to have the voice output speak each letter of a word or string the letters together to form a whole word. The user can choose to hear all the modifier keys announced (<SHIFT>, <TAB>, or <ENTER>) or have them silenced. Most leading screen-reading programs contain a number of these features, but programs vary according to producer and model. As with any product, buyers should read consumer reviews of the screen readers before making any purchasing decisions.[1]

Screen-reading software producers generally supply a variety of configurations written specifically for popular reading applications. Advanced users often further configure a speech program to suit their per-

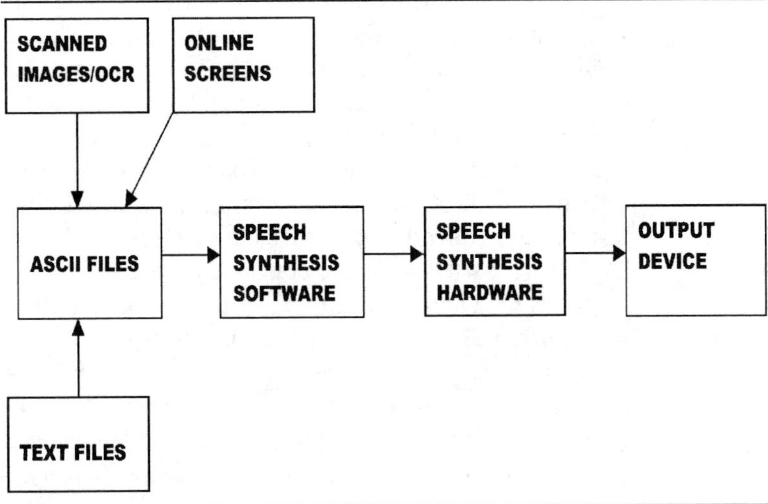

FIGURE 4-1
Basics of speech output

sonal preferences and offer their configurations free of charge at shareware sites.

Typically, current speech programs allow the reader to select whether to have just highlighted text, the whole screen, or no screen output spoken. Additionally, because important messages often appear in a particular color or position on the display screen, the screen reader can be told to monitor the screen for these messages and announce them when they appear.

Other screen-output options control such factors as whether blank lines should be spoken. Should some, most, or all punctuation be spoken? At what rate should the computer speak? How should the speech alert the user when highlighted text is encountered? Naturally, each user will have his or her favorite configuration and more than likely no two people will like the same one.

Finding the Standard Configuration for a Public Setting

A major challenge for anyone providing a publicly accessible computer system with speech output installed is finding a solution that will meet each user's individual needs or desires. Libraries are faced with the challenge of providing computer access to people who use a variety of access methods. More than half a dozen speech-output systems are being sold in the United States. Each software package has its legions of dedicated users. Screen-access and speech-output systems are quite complex to configure, learn, and use. For this reason, most computer users learn the intricacies of only one system. Therefore, when a computer user with a disability arrives at a library wishing to use the library's

Internet-connected computer, he or she may find the particular access system installed at the library a total mystery. This, of course, leads to disappointment, frustration, and often anger aimed at the library.

Several years ago, it was practical for an end user who required speech output to bring a particular system to the library and hook it up to the library's computer, thus ensuring that the user would know how to operate the computer. This worked when access involved plugging in a remote voice synthesizer and loading a screen reader from one floppy disk. This approach is no longer practical. Most screen-access programs used to access the Windows operating system require multiple disks. When they are installed, they often make basic changes to the computer software setup. Most voice synthesizers today are internal computer boards. To install one of these synthesizers requires opening the computer's case and inserting the board into one of the computer's expansion slots, if one is available. These two factors—the size of modern-day screen-access programs and the use of internal voice synthesizers—make it impractical for users to bring their own systems to a library setting.

Once a basic configuration is established that is likely to meet most users' needs, configuration of the speech software by users should not be allowed. Today, most screen readers automatically save any configurations; therefore, if a user inadvertently changes a working configuration to one that is unusable, the new configuration will be saved. This is where an advisory board comprised of members with various needs and disabilities must work with the site's automation staff to determine which settings are best for the widest range of users. In the same vein, as with settings on workstations for the nondisabled users, compromises will have to be made to serve the greatest number of users. This feature should be disabled or staff will be constantly rebooting the computers to restore the original settings.

The Cost

Voice synthesizers range in price from a low of around $200, if the computer's sound card is used, to approximately $1,000 with a specialized sound card. Often computer users who are blind or learning disabled prefer the voice synthesizer they use on a daily basis, for they are accustomed to its intonations. In an institutional setting, however, where many different users will be interfacing with the computer and screen reader, more common speech cards such as Dectalk or higher-end Creative Labs Soundblaster card will almost certainly find favor with most users.

The Dectalk and Keynote Gold systems are among the most expensive and, according to many users, produce the best-sounding speech output. Screen-reading software generally costs $500 to $700. At this price range, the software should provide access to the Windows operating system and may also provide support for disk operating system (DOS) programs. At today's prices, a complete speech-output system for a computer can be purchased for $2,000 or less.

Onward to the Internet—System Requirements

Before proceeding, the automation staff must remember that a computer with a multimedia card is not the same as speech output (a common misconception) and that the library should not provide a computer without access equipment and expect users to personalize the system as needed. So the question arises, what is needed?

First, computer hardware requirements must be considered. The computer intended as the public Internet access point that will be fitted with some form of speech output most likely is going to run Windows 95. This means the system must be at least a Pentium with a clock speed of not less than 133 MHz. It should possess 32 megabytes of Random Access Memory (RAM) with a high-quality graphics card installed. Why the need for a quality graphics card if the system is primarily going to be used for blind patrons? The answer is fairly simple. While on the Internet as well as off, today's computers constantly encounter numerous images that need to be processed and displayed. Almost all access software (screen readers) place a drag on the computer's speed. This drag plus the constant need to process graphics can, if a slow video card is installed, make the computer operate at frustratingly slow speeds. A high-performance video card is one of the least-expensive components in the computer and is an area where it is unwise to cut costs.

In summary, the basic computer system that is planned as an accessible workstation should be designed with performance and speed in mind. Adaptive add-ons such as speech synthesizers and screen readers place extra drags on the computers.

Popular Speech-Access Programs

Artic WinVision 97

Developed by Artic Technologies to navigate the Windows 95 environment, WinVision easily installs from Windows 95 and avails itself of Microsoft's Active Accessibility. WinVision works so closely with Windows that it actually installs its files into the Windows directory. The results are fewer crashes caused by conflicts in Windows when using WinVision than by other screen readers. J. D. Leventhal, Senior Resource Specialist, and C. L. Earl, Resource Specialist, Technical Evaluation Services, National Technology Center, American Foundation for the Blind (AFB), also found that WinVision granted "very good access to text-impaired users" when using Internet Explorer, but only marginal access through Netscape Navigator.[2]

The evaluators found that WinVision's command structure relied heavily on <CONTROL> and <ALT>, but the manufacturer countered with the suggestion that most users were not bothered by the need to double-click <ALT> or <CONTROL> that negated the perceived conflict that Leventhal and Earl found. Artic also pointed out that their product offered the users the opportunity to remap the keyboard (not wise in a shared setting). Another feature of WinVision's program is that it has pop-up menus so speech settings can be easily changed. This is good for the savvy user, but, again, could create a problem for the novice in a shared workstation.

A tutorial on audiocassette is available and documentation updated on an ongoing basis. Artic claims to have a close working relationship with Microsoft, Lotus, and Corel (Word Perfect) to solve current problems and prevent future conflicts. Artic Technologies does maintain a Website, but does not yet offer a demo product.[3]

Automatic Screen Access for Windows (ASAW) by MicroTalk

Automatic Screen Access for Windows (ASAW) is a system that provides blind and learning disabled computer users with "state-of-the-art speech access to applications within the Windows environment." ASAW works by gathering information displayed on the computer screen and translating it into recognizable speech through a supported speech synthesizer.

To access ASAW, the user enters commands via the numeric keypad of a conventional keyboard. The <7> reads the previous line of text and images on the screen, the <8> reads the current line, and <9> reads the next line. The middle row of numbers is used to break the line down word by word, while the bottom row of numbers breaks down the letters of the words. A tutorial is included with the package that frees staff from having to do a lot of teaching.

Commands allow the user to silence punctuation, if desired, as well as silence irrelevant information at will. ASAW also uses a high-tech image-recognition analysis algorithm that allows the user to assign names to images and announce them as such wherever and whenever they appear in the document.

When the product was reviewed by Leventhal and Earl, they concluded that "while the program was easy to install and easy to use, it lacked basic features such as 'Find,' 'Read Paragraph,' which gives the user greater control over what is spoken."[4] The reviewers also felt that the device did not perform well with Internet Explorer 3.02 or Netscape Navigator Gold 3.01 and relied too heavily on users having an "excellent knowledge of the application's use as well as good memory and reasoning skills."

The manufacturer recommends that the computer that ASAW is installed on have at least eight megabytes of RAM for use with Windows 95. The manufacturer does provide prospective clients with a free demonstration diskette that generously details the features and provides a good sense of access issues.[5]

JAWS for Windows (JFW)

JAWS for Windows (JFW), a product by the Henter-Joyce Corporation, offers the user access to a small set of basic speech commands that are enhanced by program-specific macros to access various window applications (figure 4-2). JFW "looks" at the text displayed on the screen and determines if text that appears to be on the same line actually is on that line or is "spillage" from another column.

Leventhal and Earl reviewed JFW and found it worked well with the Internet Explorer. It automatically read the first screen of a new Website as it loaded by just pressing <PAGE DOWN> and found each link (and spoke) within the site by pressing <TAB>. While used with Netscape Navigator, however, JAWS was not able to find and "speak" each link offered through the site and did not find all the graphics. It should be noted that the problem exists because of Netscape's configuration rather than that of JFW.

Leventhal and Earl found that the macros provided offered easy access to their applications, but more were needed because writing macros is beyond the capabilities of most users. If an operation has automation staff, the macros needed would be fairly easy to write.

Henter-Joyce's JAWS had the honor of being added to the Permanent Research Collection of Information Technology at the Smithsonian National Museum of American History in 1999 as it was deemed a product which utilizes new technology for the benefit of society.

Henter-Joyce's product comes with a tutorial and quick reference guide and tollfree technical assistance. A demonstration copy of new and updated products is available on the Henter-Joyce Website.[6]

FIGURE 4-2
JAWS for Windows

SLIMWARE Windows Bridge

SLIMWARE Windows Bridge is a product of Syntha-Voice Computers, a Canadian company headquartered in Ontario, with U.S. offices in Niagara Falls, New York, that is popular with North American users. The product allows the user to "feel at home" within the graphical environment of Microsoft's Windows by using the same access commands for navigation (a plus for staff and patrons alike) while using the Syntha-Voice product.

A big plus is that Windows Bridge contains a Mouse Search command that allows the user to instantly move the mouse pointer to a specific location such as an icon or menu selection. It also helps the user find edit boxes and aids in orientation and perception requirements by telling the user how far he or she has moved through a document and the size of the items at the current location.

The product also includes an Icon Label Library, which contains descriptive labels for more than 1,000 commonly used Windows icons, as well as a feature that allows the user to "point" at any icon on the screen and instantly receive a descriptive label for the image.

Another advantage is that the product works with 40 popular synthesizers including Soundblaster. Commands can be given to have the reader announce punctuation, window titles, buttons, graphic frames, prompts, submenus, and dialogue boxes.

According to the evaluation by Leventhal and Earl, SLIMWARE Windows Bridge provided good access to both the Internet Explorer and Netscape Navigator. The program contains many rewritten configurations and hotkeys that give the experienced user quick access to Internet functions. In addition, while accessing Netscape Navigator and Internet Explorer with SLIMWARE and pressing a hotkey and <PAGE DOWN>, the text impaired reader will be able to read the first screen of a new Web page and the following pages.

Leventhal and Earl felt that SLIMWARE was best suited for advanced users, for its sophisticated features allow skilled users to greatly improve its performance in complex applications. They felt that beginners would have difficulty with the program. Syntha-Voice countered this criticism by pointing out that allowance is given to redesign commands using the Bridge's "online Help Mode." Syntha-Voice does offer a complimentary demo program through its home page.[7]

MasterTouch

A product of HumanWare products, MasterTouch's claim to fame is that it allows the "user to monitor all or selected screen changes as they occur without the need to suspend the application and review the screen." Promotional material states that command keys can be redefined by the user and that configurations for specialized applications can be instantly retrieved. HumanWare includes a training guide in print, disk, and on cassette; additionally, an online, context-sensitive Help module is included.

The strongest selling point for MasterTouch, however, is that it will work on a wide variety of personal computer (PC) networks.

V Voice for OPACs

TeleSensory Products realized the importance of developing a product that would allow users who are visually impaired or learning disabled to "listen to the OPAC" and other online materials provided by public libraries. TeleSensory sought out the major library vendors and asked what the company needed to do to make a product that would work in conjunction with the operating software. The answer to giving voice to the catalogs was V Voice.

V Voice works much the same as other screen-reader programs. Adjustments to the displays are executed with keystroke commands. The software comes with headphones, external speaker, and instructional manual. V Voice works with V View, a screen-enlarging product, and can be installed on the same terminal, a major plus.

This product works with many automated systems used by libraries, but not all; check with the software supplier about the compatibility. Telesensory does offer a free demonstration of the product.[8]

Window-Eyes

Manufactured by GW Micro Inc., Window-Eyes is a moderately priced screen reader that works with an extended 101 keyboard, with the number pad emulating mouse commands. The ACT Center at the University of Missouri-Columbia reviewed the product and found that it was "reliable, stable, and intelligent."[9] The commands are easy to remember and there is no need to develop complex macros (which makes learning easier for the novice), although it is possible to define 50 standard and ten Hyperactive Windows. The Hyperactive Windows will announce changes as they appear in defined regions.

The reviewers found that Window-Eyes did a good job with Netscape when using the standard Windows applications rather than the hotkeys designed to access the page and noted that this was the case wherever problems occurred.

Popular Speech Synthesizers

The questions most often asked when discussing speech access to information are, "How good are speech synthesizers and how much do they cost?" Because speech synthesizers are programmed to work with a highly complex set of phonetic rules (as opposed to words), terms and personal names are often pronounced in confusing and amusing manners, for the English language does not follow standard rules of phonetics.

The price range is a wide one, with the less-expensive units sounding more mechanical and the more-expensive units allotting the user a choice of nine different voices. Much as a person perks up a little when he or she hears a voice reminiscent of pleasant people and times and cringes when he or she hears a voice that does the opposite, speech synthesizers are usually a matter of personal taste. The main thing to look for when choosing a synthesizer is compatibility with the screen reader, for the user will eventually get used to the voice. Note: Synthesizers are available as internal or external peripherals; institutional settings should install the synthesizer internally because there is less chance for manipulation (intentional or unintentional) and theft.

DecTalk

DecTalk (a product of Digital Equipment Corporation) text-to-speech utility provides the user with a wide range of predefined voices (four male, four female, and one child) who "speak" at a rate of 75 to 650 words per minute. DecTalk is programmed with an extensive set of rules to provide greater accuracy of spoken text and proper names. Additionally, there are controls for pauses, pitch, and stress, as well as allowances for homographs. Digital does interface well with most screen readers and is available in several languages. DecTalk is one of the higher-priced, high-quality synthesizers. However, it is the most widely used in the business world and is generally the easiest to understand by new users.

SynPhonix

Artic's SynPhonix synthesizer is one of the originals in the artificial speech market. It provides the user with the ability to use hotkeys to adjust the pitch and rate of speed at which the text is spoken. Users find that the speech is crisp and the response is quick. The review keys are easy to manipulate and allow the users to spell the words they do not understand. The SynPhonix synthesizer follows an extensive set of rules to pronounce words.

Keynote Gold

HumanWare is the manufacturer of Keynote Gold, a high-end speech synthesizer. Designed to cope with the inconsistencies of the English language, it adjusts to 16 pitch levels and a reading rate of 50 to 500 words per minute. It supports a wide variety of screen readers and enables the user to enter commands independently of the keyboard through a Touch Tablet. The Keynote Gold offers several language options.

GW Micro's Sounding Board

GW Micro's Sounding Board provides the user with a responsive, cost-effective, quality synthesizer. While the product does not offer the user so many options as other synthesizers do, it is acceptable to an audience of various users at different levels of "listening" to artificial voices.

Screen Readers and the Windows Issue

Over the past ten years, issues surrounding the development of software to produce speech or Braille output for blind and learning disabled computer users have become very complicated. The factor contributing most to this complexity is the switch from text-based to graphics-based computer systems. As programmers of today's Windows systems attempt to make computer usage easier and easier for people watching the screen through the use of graphics or symbols, they are, at the same time, making it more and more difficult for the programmers of access systems to produce software that can accurately read the screen.

Entire books and speeches have been written concerning the problems blind people experience using the Windows interface. The use of buttons, scroll bars, wheels, and other nontextual symbols can, indeed, make it very difficult for a blind computer user to navigate through a list of choices. Likewise for the computer users with learning disabilities, trying to interpret the meanings of the items they see can be equally as difficult and aggravating. The less-disciplined from these user groups may end up abandoning their treks onto the information highway out of sheer frustration.

The Internet, in particular, can offer a multitude of clever symbols and icons meant to be intuitive to the eye but often obscure to the screen-reading software. No matter what system a public library, university, or any other organization sets up that is intended to provide speech access to the Internet, there will always be Internet sites that cannot be interpreted by screen-reading programs and the alternative "sighted reader" may be needed to interpret what the screen reader cannot.

The Internet—Unique Access Issues

Because there is often confusion regarding the population's conceptual definition of "the Internet" and "the Web," it is necessary to first define what is meant by the word *Internet* versus the word *Web*. The Internet, as defined in Chapter 1, is the actual interconnectivity of computer-based information resources around the world. A variety of methods facilitate communications between these computer systems. Electronic mail is one of the most popular ways for individuals and businesses to use the Internet. When a patron of a library wants to know if he or she can gain access to the Internet at the library, however, it is quite likely that the question is really, Does the library have Web access? This term, the

Web, has come to stand for a particular way people use to search for information or enjoy multimedia presentations on the Internet. The Web is an underpinning for the common term the *Web browser.*

Browsers

To gain access to information on the Internet that is stored and transmitted over the Web, a computer must have a software package designed to match the requirements of the Web. Popular browsers are Netscape, Internet Explorer, Spyglass, Lynx, and Net-Tamer. Lynx and Net-Tamer are called text browsers because they do not have the inherent ability to show graphics and can run in a nongraphical environment. Web browsers will explore the entire Internet; that is, they are not limited to information that is placed on Web-coded pages.

While it is not difficult to install multiple browsers, it is difficult for staff to remember how to use the accessible browsers in addition to all the standards from reference searches.

While textual information is pretty much the same on or off the Internet, it is the multimedia features of the Internet that make it a unique setting for access systems. Will patrons want to access the multimedia aspect of the Web? The answer is a resounding *Yes*! especially the audio or sound capabilities of the Internet. Therefore, the Internet access computer should be equipped with a browser that allows the user to play Internet audio, and the screen-reading system should not be tied to the computer sound card unless the screen reader is designed to allow the sound card to play audio.

The most popular screen-reading programs can work with the popular Soundblaster audio card. While the screen reader is operating, however, the sound card generally cannot perform other audio functions that the computer may request. This means that if the screen reader is using the computer's sound card to produce the actual speech, it may not be possible to hear any audio from the Internet. Therefore, the computer's audio card cannot be used alone and a separate speech synthesizer is required.

Choosing which browser(s) to use as the Internet access system for a library's patrons is an important decision.

Unfortunately, selecting an Internet browser is not a decision that can be made independently of the screen reader. Both the access system and the browser selected for Internet access must be considered together. The various choices for combinations of Internet and screen-reading software are many but are not unlimited.

The Most Basic Browser—the Shell Account

The most basic Internet access is to use a screen reader and a modem with a communications package to connect to an Internet provider with what is referred to as a shell account. In this situation, the user runs only the communications package on the workstation. All Internet access is provided by the Internet service. This is an inexpensive, uncomplicated way to gain quick access to text on the Internet. Audio or other multimedia features of the Internet are not available. Shell accounts are becoming harder to find as more and more providers move to the "direct connect" Point to Point Protocol (PPP) or a Serial Line Interface Protocol (SLIP) Internet access. In these situations, the provider furnishes a connection to the Internet, but the Internet access software is run on the workstation. Files that are retrieved come directly to the workstation and all multimedia features can be made available.

Lynx: Text-Based Browser

Lynx is a text browser that combined with a DOS-based screen reader will offer basic Internet service to the user. This is a plus for a tight budget because this low-cost approach can be run on a fairly low-powered system. This is important for those still using a SLIP or PPP connection or having a connection to the Internet through a local area network that is DOS- rather than Unix-based. Lynx is available free of charge from the University of Kansas. The compiled program (all the original programming code and the documentation) can be downloaded by anyone with an Internet connection.[10]

The disadvantages of Lynx are many and quite severe. The multimedia capabilities would not be available and the patron would have to be taught the specific screen-reader package being used. Lynx also uses a system that interferes with other operations because the commands to move the pointer or cursor around are <J> and <K> to move up or down on the screen and <H> and <L> to move it left or right. The <L> actually activates a link; <H> takes the user back one link.

Although tedious, this works until the user needs to fill in a form or answer questions that require using these letters—it cannot be done.

Another disadvantage of Lynx is that this browser is not well known among the general users and instructions will need to be given. Staff will need at least a rudimentary knowledge of the browser and detailed instructions in a usable medium will need to be developed, for it is unlikely that anyone in the library will have experience running it.

Windows-Based Browsers

The two most-popular Windows browsers in this category are Netscape and Internet Explorer. Before either of these browsers can be operated by a blind or learning disabled computer user, good access to the Windows operating system itself must be achieved. At present, several Windows screen readers are available. Without exception, no screen reader gives access to Windows or the Internet to the same degree that is obtained by visually watching and comprehending what is displayed on the screen.

Programmers are striving to make the Internet browsers more useful for people using adaptive technologies and progress is being made. And Microsoft has given some attention to helping screen-reader producers develop better access to its popular Explorer program.

It is altruistic to say there are no disadvantages to establishing a public-access workstation with a Windows-based screen reader. The main problem is that screen readers are complex. A user may be well versed in one program and not have any idea how to operate another one. Very possibly, no matter which screen reader is selected, users will have to be trained on using the screen reader before they can learn to access the Internet. The advantages do outweigh the disadvantages: First, there will be full multimedia access, and second, sighted colleagues may be able to provide some assistance, at least with the operation of the mainstream browser.

Keep in mind that sighted computer users who are not familiar with the operation of Windows-based screen readers are often unable to assist a blind user because the blind user depends on keystroke navigation while the sighted computer operator generally uses a mouse to navigate.

Lynx for Windows

A unique group of programs called console applications has been developed that often work better for blind computer operators than pure Windows programs do. One such program is Lynx for Windows, which has all the advantages of a text browser, but it can be easily linked with other applications in Windows so the user can experience multimedia presentations on the Web.

The Lynx program has several features that make it an ideal browser for persons using Braille, speech, or large print. For example, a command line option "-show_cursor" when typed after the Lynx command causes the terminal's cursor to follow the pointer as it moves from link to link. This feature means that the Braille or speech output always shows what link is being pointed to. The navigation keys can be the same as the computer's cursor key. The Down arrow takes the user to the next link; the Up arrow moves the user up the screen one link. The Right arrow activates the link that is being pointed to, while the Left arrow goes back one link.

The Options menu also allows a user to choose between numbered or unnumbered links. When numbered links are selected, a user can read a screen and pick the option by simply pressing the number of that option and pressing Enter. Also from the Options menu, the user can select his or her level of expertise (from novice to expert), which allows the user to explore and learn at his or her own pace. For example, in the expert mode, the user is able to fixate the address of the linked document on the bottom of the screen, allowing the user to quickly find the link.

One facet of Lynx that may be of use for the home browser may actually cause a problem for a computer that will be used by a myriad of people, and that is the ability to easily personalize a program for a specific user. Lynx allows the user to add bookmarks of his or her own simply by pressing <A> and to retrieve them by pressing the <V>. Allowing users to do this will cause more problems for the administrators of the site than the advantages persons with disabilities would gain from enabling them. Thus, this feature should be disabled.

While using the Lynx program, a user cannot view images or maps. These files can, however, be downloaded to a hard disk and viewed later. For people browsing the Web with speech or Braille, image viewing may not be a serious concern. Related to this issue, however, is having the ability to hear sound files online. The Lynx user must always download the audio file and play it with a sound utility.

If the computer used to access the Internet is used only for that purpose, then a knowledgeable computer-support person can configure the system so no Windows screen reader is needed. The Lynx for Windows requires only a DOS screen reader.

Dedicated Web Browsers

Adaptive is the word that appears with the greatest frequency in this work and is used to describe the methods a person with disabilities uses to access products designed for nondisabled persons. But as noted there will be times when even the most sophisticated, accurate screen reader will require human intervention. Recently, however, products have been developed specifically to make access to the Web easier for persons who must use or prefer keyboard commands to surf the Net.

PwWebSpeak is the best-known product in this category of dedicated Web browsers. This browser program provides full keyboard navigation.[11] Additionally, any page's structure and content will be spoken using pwWebSpeak's utility. Contrary to other screen-reader and synthesizer combinations, because this program provides its own speech output, no other screen reader is required as long as Internet access is all that is desired. Note: If the PC will be used for any other application, the previously mentioned applications must be installed.

Additionally, this program supports simultaneous large-print, onscreen displays with full control of size, foreground, and background colors. This is helpful to persons with low vision, persons with learning disabilities, and persons with vision problems such as color blindness. These modifications are accomplished with simple keystrokes. For instance, <SHIFT F11> increases the print size each time it is pressed until the user finds a usable size; <CTRL F12> cycles through a palette of background colors until the usable one is found; <SHIFT F12> cycles through a palette of foreground colors until a usable one is found.

The commands used in pwWebSpeak are simple and sensible. For instance, the space bar is used to bring up the home page and used throughout the program (<ENTER> is also used and the user must listen to the prompt) to make a choice, go to a link, start a Web search, etc.; <F1> is used as the Help command; <F10> will read a Page Summary identifying the number of links, headers, images, image maps, and forms; <ALT F10> will prod the reader to speak the URL of the current page, while pressing <F11> twice will spell the URL.

The browser allows for easy opening, closing, and saving of Web pages. Reading and navigating the Web pages is also facilitated by easy keystroke commands. The F3 command will make the browser read the current Web page from its current position to its conclusion; lowercase <q> will make the browser stop reading or stop the Web page transfer; lowercase <a> moves the user to the next link on the page.

Another plus of this program is that it allows the user to use the key commands to adjust the synthesizer volume (if one is included) and play back a real audio clip, if it is stored at the sound level needed.

This interface is intuitive and easy to teach a new user. But remember to always include easy-to-follow instructions at the workstation in an appropriate usable media.

Other Issues

Large-Print Keytops

These press-ply labels are an aid for persons with learning disabilities using the voice access to the computer as well as those users with low vision. The letters fill the entire key, thus assuring that fingers are resting on the row that the user intended them to be on. These labels will withstand public usage and can be viewed on the Hooleon Website.[12]

Location and Signage

While it may seem thoughtful to locate the workstation in a private area of the facility, this should be avoided. Try to find a central location for the workstation to enable patrons to locate it without help. Persons with low vision or learning disabilities may not be able to follow complicated directions on how to get to a location of the workstation located three-quarters of the way through the library and to the right and then the left. If it is not possible to locate the terminal in an accessible place, patrons should be escorted to a location that will allow them to find the station.

Signage should be easy to read for those with vision. Calligraphy and fonts with serifs can be very difficult for some patrons with learning disabilities. Professional fonts can be used that will look good and be easy to use such as HP Presentations or CG Times Bold.

Training—a Brief Reminder

Do not expect that most blind or learning disabled individuals who come into a library will already know how to use a computer or how to use the particular type of access hardware and software that the library offers. It will be necessary to provide documentation in special formats for these users, as well as offering frequent training and familiarization sessions. If tutorials are not available, ask the consumer advisory panel to develop one for use with the products.

It may be helpful to draw on the experiences of other libraries using similar equipment or to utilize the services of a consultant in the community who is familiar with a particular setup. The formation of a formally trained, on-call volunteer corps to teach new users is also a plus, for paid staff available to train new users are usually scarce. Tutorials often are available on tape, thus placing a tape player near a computer with speech output may also help.

While facilitated-speech access can be difficult at times, it is also rewarding. Once the configurations are made and the training completed, staff and users alike will embrace the new technology and access possibilities.

Notes

1. Screen readers reviews may be found at <www.utoronto.ca/atrc/rd/library/papers/consumer.html>, as well as in publications written for and by people with disabilities. Good choices for practical and nonpartisan reviews include "Closing the Gap," "Tactic," and "JVIB News Service."
2. J. D. Leventhal and C. L. Earl, "A Review of Two Speech Access Programs for Windows 95: SLIMWARE Window Bridge and WinVision," *Journal of Visual Impairment and Blindness* (April 1998): 242–44.
3. Contact Artic Technologies, 55 Park Street, Troy, MI 48083; or call (248) 588-7370; or visit their Website at <www.artictech.com>.
4. For a complete review of this product, please see J. D. Leventhal and C. L. Earl, "A Review of Two Speech Access Programs for Windows 95: ASAW and JAWS for Windows," *Journal of Visual Impairment and Blindness* (November-December 1997): 17–19.
5. To obtain a trial diskette, contact the manufacturer: MicroTalk Software Inc., 721 Olive Street, Texarkana, TX 75501; or e-mail <larry@screenaccess.com>; or visit their Website at <www.screenaccess.com>.
6. To receive a copy of the diskette, contact Henter-Joyce, Inc., at (800) 336-5658; or e-mail <info@hj.com>; or visit their Website at <hj.com>.
7. Contact Syntha-Voice at Syntha-Voice Computers, 300 Queenston Road, Suite 394, Stoney Creek, ON L8G IA7, Canada; or call (800) 263-4540; or visit their Website at <www.synthavoice.on.ca>.
8. Contact TeleSensory Systems, 520 Almanor Avenue, Sunnyvale, CA 94081-3533; or call (800) 804-8004, (408) 616-8700, or (408) 616-8720; or visit their Website at <www.telesensory.com>.
9. "Window-Eyes 1.05," University of Missouri-Columbia ACT Center Product Reviews. Review date November 12, 1996, found at <www.missouri.edu/~ccact/prodrev>.
10. The address for the browser is <ftp2.cc.ukans.edu/pub/DosLynx>. Remember, it is always wise to run any piece of shareware through a virus check before installing it on your hard drive, for it may have picked up a virus through constant access.

11. John C. DeWitt and Markku Hakkinen, "Surfing the Web with pwWebSpeak." DeWitt & Associates, Midland Park, New Jersey and Productivity Works, Inc. (Paper presented at the 1998 CSUN Conference sponsored by California State University, Northridge, Center on Disabilities, March 1998).
12. More information can be obtained about the keytops by contacting Hooleon at Hooleon Corporation, 411 South 6th Street, Building B, Cottonwood, AZ 86326; or call (520) 634-4503 or (800) 937-1337; or visit their Website at <www. hooleon.com>.

5

Touching the Internet with Braille

After learning why speech access to PCs and the Internet is economical as well as user-friendly, you may feel the need to ask the questions, "Why do blind people still use Braille when they could just flip the <SPEECH ACCESS> and listen?" and "Why should we explore, purchase, and install Braille systems in our facilities when so few people read Braille?"

Judith M. Dixon, Consumer Relations Officer, National Library Service (NLS) for the Blind and Physically Handicapped, the Library of Congress, explains the basics of Braille, why access should be offered, as well as what is feasible. She also outlines the factors librarians should consider when developing an access strategy.

Nowhere are economic realities more of a factor than when planning to provide Braille access. While access to computers and the Internet with Braille can and should be part of any overall access plan, librarians can become discouraged when considering Braille because Braille equipment is significantly more expensive than its speech or large-print counterparts, and the literature is replete with references to how few people can actually read Braille.

The Basics of Braille

Braille is a tactile code that enables blind persons to read and write. It was invented by a blind Frenchman, Louis Braille, in 1829. Traditionally, Braille is embossed by hand or machine onto heavy paper and read by moving a person's fingers across the top of the dots.

The Braille code comprises a rectangular six-dot cell that is three dots high and two dots wide, with up to 63 possible combinations using one or more of the six dots. Dots are numbered from top to bottom in the Braille cell—one, two, and three on the left, and four, five, and six on the right. Braille only has one set of letters. By itself, a Braille letter is assumed to be lowercase. To indicate that a letter is uppercase, another Braille cell (the capital sign, dot six) must precede it. To show an uppercase word, two capital signs are put in front of the word. The number sign, dots three-four-five-six, preceding a letter makes it a number.

Many more symbols are in print than the 63 Braille symbols can represent. Most computer systems, for example, handle 96 different symbols. To show a wider variety of symbols in Braille, two or more Braille cells are combined for each symbol.

To reduce the bulkiness of books and other documents, Braille uses a system of contractions, or abbreviations. A Braille contraction is a combination of one or more cells used to shorten the length of a word. The word *mother* in Braille, for instance, would be represented by a contraction occupying only two cells rather than by spelling out the whole six-letter word.

There are several grades of Braille. Grade-1 Braille does not contain any contractions, but it does represent capitalization, numbers, and punctuation with the correct Braille symbols. Grade-1 Braille is used only for specialized applications where the Braille contractions might be confusing, such as in spelling lists. Grade-2 Braille is the most common form in North America and uses nearly 200 different contractions to represent capitalization, numbers, and punctuation marks. See figure 5-1 for samples of each Braille grade.

Who Uses Braille?

Braille is used by blind persons or persons whose vision is sufficiently impaired so they cannot read printed material. Braille is an extremely efficient and reliable tool of literacy for blind persons. Like a print reader, a Braille reader is aware of the spelling and punctuation of words in a document; it is the closest approximation to print for blind persons.

Braille also enables a blind person to write in a form that can be immediately read. With simple devices, Braille can be punched by hand, and rugged mechanical Braille typewriters are readily available and widely used by Braille readers. Blind persons of all ages and in all walks of life use Braille in the same ways that sighted persons use print.

Learning to read Braille is much the same process as learning to read print, using touch rather than sight to distinguish the symbols. The best readers of Braille learned it as children, but many motivated adults have also become excellent Braille readers.

One of the most common statistics available on using Braille is that only 10 percent of the blind population reads Braille. On examination, however, two factors make this statistic difficult to interpret. First, the

Recorded and brailled books are available, free, to anyone who is unable to read conventional inkprint because of a visual or physical handicap.

Grade 1 Braille

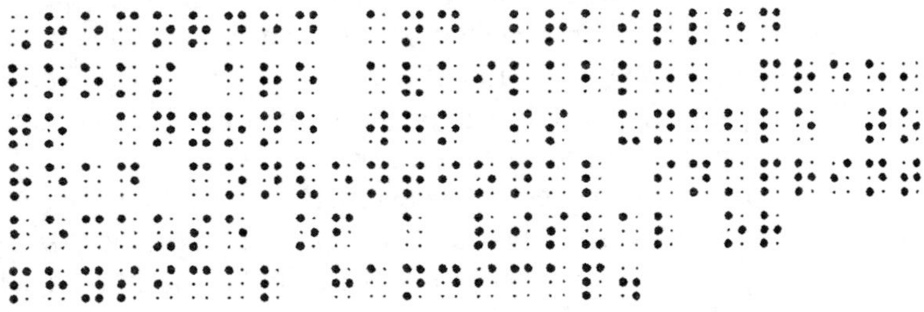

Grade 2 Braille

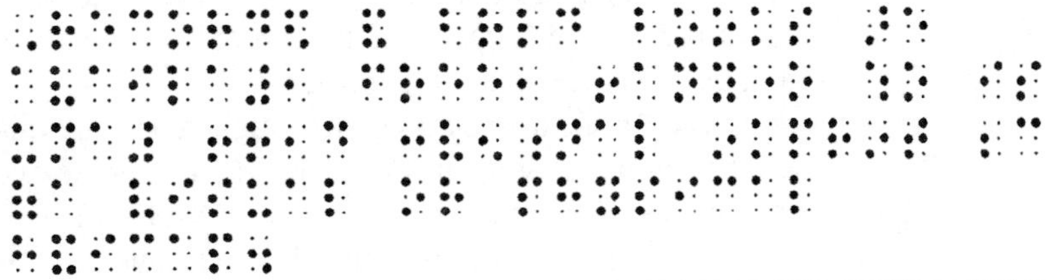

FIGURE 5-1

Sample sentence written in conventional type and in Grade-1 and Grade-2 Braille

entire blind population on which it is based includes people with widely varying visual abilities. In 1985, a study of totally blind people found that 50 percent of that population could read Braille. Another more recent study conducted by the AFB found that 93 percent of totally blind, employed persons could read Braille.[1]

Second, the statistic does not address what "read Braille" means. Does it mean that the reader must be proficient enough to read an entire book? Would someone who can read a Braille label or a telephone number in Braille qualify as a Braille reader? Even an individual with somewhat limited Braille fluency can find Braille access beneficial.

Also, for the small population that is deaf-blind, Braille is the only means to access "printed" information.

Braille Displays for Computer Access

While speech output currently has the widest appeal among adaptive interfaces, for many blind computer users who are efficient Braille readers, a Braille display is the preferred interface because of the inherent high level of information and detail. Braille displays provide access to the information on a computer screen by converting standard ASCII text into Braille. In response to information from the computer, Braille is produced on the display by pins that are raised and lowered (refreshed) in combinations to form Braille characters (see figure 5-2). When used with screen-access programs, Braille displays allow users to access any portion of the screen information. All Braille displays in the United States today can show only one line of Braille and are commonly available in 20-, 40-, or 80-character Braille-cell configurations. Some displays are portable and battery-powered, while others are larger desktop units that typically sit under the computer keyboard.

For a good Braille reader, the use of a Braille display can offer many benefits over other access modalities. A Braille display allows the user to move quickly from one point on the screen to any other; to skip large blank spaces easily; to watch an item on the screen change rather than having to query the screen for the latest update; to read at a personal, often variable, rate; to observe many specifics about the text such as spelling, punctuation, and format; and to be keenly aware of items on the screen and their relative position to one another.

The Braille display must accurately represent what is being shown on the computer's screen. To do this, there must be one screen character per Braille cell. Therefore, most Braille displays use a special eight-dot Braille code instead of the usual six-dot Braille cell. The presence of the additional two dots per cell allows the display to show highlighted or otherwise enhanced items. This strategy, however, does not require the user to learn a completely new Braille code.

The displayed text is usually uncontracted and written in what is called "computer Braille." Computer Braille refers to a Braille code developed by the Braille Authority of North America (BANA). This code was developed so that computer-generated symbols such as the backslash or vertical bar not normally found in Braille can be represented. Some, even experienced Braille readers, may be unfamiliar with computer Braille and will need to learn a few new characters before becoming comfortable using

FIGURE 5-2
Refreshable Braille display

a Braille display. Braille displays only provide output. The blind person uses a standard keyboard to communicate with the computer.

Considerations for Including a Braille Display in a Workstation

Braille interfaces are quite expensive and most appropriate for libraries with many blind patrons. Librarians who are thinking of installing Braille interfaces should consider the following points when selecting the most appropriate equipment for the circumstances.

Size

Braille displays vary in size. The smallest display on the market today is 18 cells, while the largest ones are more than 80 cells. A larger number of cells means that the user can read more of the computer screen at any one time without moving the Braille line to another portion of the screen. A direct and dramatic relationship exists between the number of cells and the price of the display. A 40-cell display may represent a good economic compromise of offering Braille access without an enormous expense, while an 80-cell display could be a wonderful method of access for serious, frequent users.

Interface

Different models of Braille displays vary considerably in the way they will interface to a computer. Most have at least a standard serial connection, but some have an additional parallel interface option, and a few require a proprietary, internal card. Which of these is the most appropriate for the library will depend solely on the hardware configuration and what ports or slots might be available.

Software

The software that controls the Braille display varies considerably from model to model. This will be difficult for librarians to evaluate. Librarians should seek input from Braille readers regarding the most appropriate control software for the Braille display.

Most Braille displays come with software, but sometimes additional software is needed. Additional software requirements will be based on the operating system of the computer, the configuration of the network, and other similar factors.

Other Features

Some Braille displays offer a variety of specialized features such as a split screen (the ability to read a segment of the screen on one portion of the

Braille line and a completely separate portion of the screen on another part of the same line); online Braille translation; cursor routing buttons; and many more. Here again, which features are appropriate for each library will depend on the requirements of the users and the type of library.

Popular Braille Displays

ALVA

ALVA, which is made in Sweden and resold by HumanWare, offers the Braille user a 45- or 85-dot Braille-cell display that constantly shows the user exactly where he or she is all the time. The display not only tells the user where the cursor is, but it also will relay which screen attributes are active (highlighting, location of cursor).

ALVA requires very little training because it works through an intuitive menuing system. ALVA will work with Windows 95.

Braille Window Refreshable Display

The Braille Window from HumanWare is a powerful refreshable display that "empowers Braille readers to navigate easily through Windows 95 or 3.x with fewer keystrokes and more confidence." The desktop model has an 85 eight-dot cell display with six programmable "touch cursors" as well as five cells that monitor "status information" for locating information as it appears on the display screen. The firmware is stored in Read-Only Memory (ROM), which ensures a more stable operation and less chances of disruption of other programs. Braille Window also works without conflict in a speech-access program such as JAWS.

Braille Embossers for Printing Output

Braille access to a computer generally refers to using a refreshable Braille display. As previously described, the refreshable Braille display provides immediate interpretation of what is being displayed on the screen. Braille access to a computer, and thus to the Internet, should also include the ability to copy and retain Web pages and documents retrieved from the Internet.

The best vehicle for output is a Braille embosser. Some libraries, however, do not allow printing and instead encourage patrons to copy material to floppy disks. When this is the case, file-format preferences should be set carefully. Blind patrons will want material copied as flat ASCII files that will work with whatever adaptive programs they normally use.

A Braille embosser (and the software to support it) should be provided at each workstation with a Braille display or speech-output device. If the embosser does not have Braille control keys, Braille overlays can be added to make independent operation simpler.

A Braille embosser can be used to print a hard copy of search results or text files. Many blind people prefer to have a hard copy of materials just as sighted users do. The price of Braille embossers has dropped significantly in recent years, and if the budget allows, a Braille embosser can provide limited Braille access, even when a Braille display is not possible.

Several factors should be taken into account when purchasing an embosser. The first is the financial resources available to the library. Braille embossers range in price from $1,500 to $35,000. The primary difference among embossers is speed and durability. At the low end of the price range, Braille embossers such as the PortaThiel or Braille Blazer produce Braille at a rate of about 18 characters per second, while at the high end, the full-size Thiel or the Braille Express can emboss at speeds in excess of 200 characters per second.

The second major difference among embossers is single-sided versus double-sided (interpoint) embossing. Interpoint embossing offers the advantage of conserving paper and reducing the bulkiness of a Braille printout. Until recently, the ability to emboss on both sides of a page simultaneously was reserved for the most expensive embossers. Several manufacturers of Braille embossers, however, now produce interpoint embossers that cost in the $3,000 to $4,000 price range and emboss at speeds of around 40 characters per second. Although the initial setup of one of these interpoint embossers can be a little tricky, the good news is that they're very reliable and generally require little maintenance.

Popular Braille Printers—Low to Midrange

Braille Blazer

The Braille Blazer (product of Blazie Engineering), one of the lowest-priced printers, will fit into the workspace allotted to a standard laser printer. It has a built-in speech synthesizer that allows the user to configure printing needs. As a bonus, the Braille Blazer can be used as a voice output for IBM-compatible PCs. The Blazer (see figure 5-3) embosses single-sided 8½"× 11" tractor-feed paper at 15 characters per second (this is very slow compared to the time it takes to print text). The Blazer embosses graphics, landscapes, and labels, a great feature if you plan to label your audiovisual collection.

Index Basic-D and Index Basic-S

Both the Index Basic-D and the Index Basic-S printers produce excellent quality Braille in a relatively easy process. The steps simply include threading the continuous-form, tractor-feed paper through the guide and toggling a few buttons. The Basic-D model is faster (300 pages per hour)

FIGURE 5-3
Braille embosser

and will print on both sides of the paper (computer Braille paper is approximately .04 of an inch thick).

The Basic-S model prints at a rate of 150 pages per hour and will print on only one side of the page. Both printers are available from Sighted Electronics.

Romeo (RB-25 and RB-40) and Juliet Interpoint and ET Braille Printers

Despite their saccharine names, the Romeo, Juliet, and ET printers provide the user with an embosser capable of rendering good-quality Braille. The Romeo 25 is the least expensive model and produces Braille at the rate of 25 characters per second; the Romeo 40 produces Braille at a rate of 40 characters per second (the price difference is about $1,000).

The Juliet Brailler prints at the rate of 40 characters per second and is capable of rendering graphics and handling paper that is 15 inches wide. The Juliet is unique because it will handle single-sheet feed, thus saving paper.

ET's design was based on the Juliet model in respect to embossing quality and speed. The difference between the ET and the Juliet is that ET will emboss at 60 characters per second on a 40-character line.

Braille Software Translators

Another aspect of producing Braille from the Internet that needs attention is the issue of Braille translation, i.e., output in computer Braille, Grade-

1, or Grade-2 Braille (see figure 5-4). An embosser can generally produce either computer Braille or Grade-1 Braille without any additional software. When text is transmitted to an embosser by simply hitting <PRINT SCREEN>, computer Braille is the result. Very few Braille readers are comfortable reading computer Braille on paper. Not only are all the words fully spelled out, but most punctuation marks and other special symbols are quite different from what is normally found in embossed books.

To produce the Braille code familiar to all experienced Braille readers, i.e., Grade 2, Braille-translation software is required. If a library decides to provide Grade-2 formatted documents, the selection of a translator

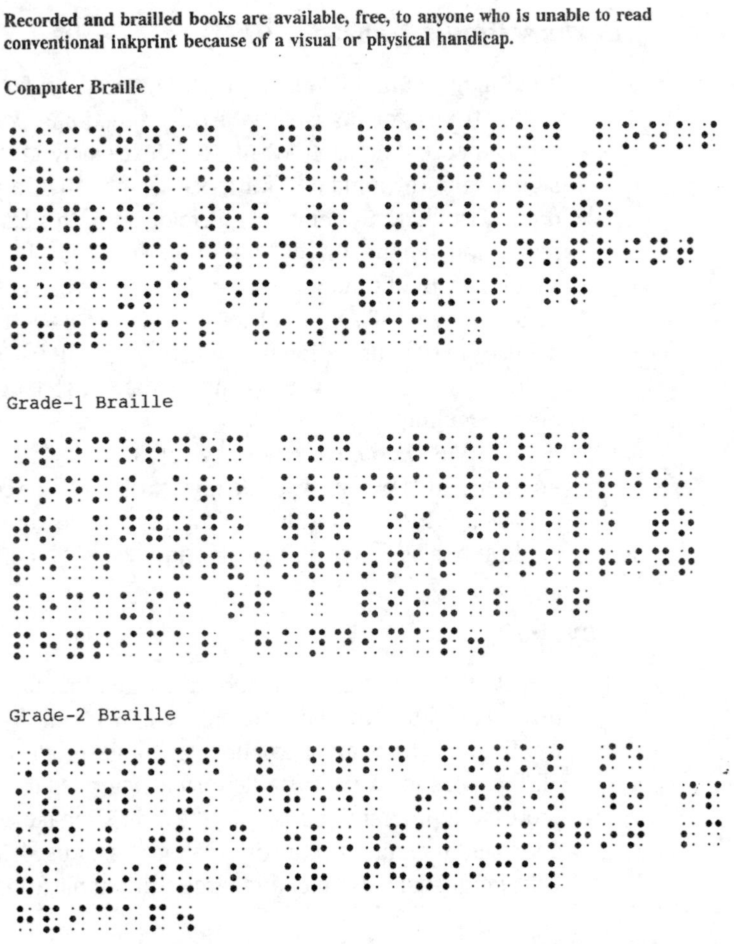

Recorded and brailled books are available, free, to anyone who is unable to read conventional inkprint because of a visual or physical handicap.

Computer Braille

Grade-1 Braille

Grade-2 Braille

FIGURE 5-4

Sample sentence written in conventional type, in computer Braille and in Grade-1 and Grade-2 Braille

depends on several factors. First, is anyone on the staff already familiar with a particular translator? Is there a local supplier of the software who can assist with installation and setup? Is someone on staff in a position to learn the procedure for producing translated Braille? It is seldom possible to simply take a document downloaded from the Internet, send it through a Braille translator, and emboss it without encountering noticeable formatting problems. To produce Grade-2 Braille generally requires the intervention of someone with knowledge of the software translator being used and the rules of Braille production (this can be self-taught with tutorials and a well-documented instruction manual).

Two Braille translators are worthy of note: the Duxbury Braille Translator (DBT) and the MegaDots.

Duxbury Braille Translator (DBT)

The Duxbury Braille Translator (DBT), shown in figure 5-5, is a complete Braille translator (as well as a fully functional word-processing device that supports Microsoft Word). It is extremely easy to use for both the sighted and the blind and for those who know Braille and for those who do not. Duxbury Systems, the developers of this translator, enjoy a good reputation among Braille users for the firm's integrity of translation. Duxbury's Braille Editor allows the user to import and translate large files, with virtually no limit to the file size. Easy-to-follow, logical steps are used in the translation process, which result in excellent Braille output for the novice. Duxbury also can translate in 15 languages and, uniquely, operates bilingually.

DBT is devoted to rendering service to its customers and maintains an informative Website with demonstrations of the company's product, as well as links to many quality disability-related sites. DBT will work with applications such as voice output and refreshable Braille.[2]

MegaDots

MegaDots is also a user-friendly software program designed for easy use by both sighted and blind users. It is a menu-driven program created to eliminate frustration for novice Braille producers. MegaDots knows all the rules for correct Braille formatting. MegaDots is in itself a word-processing program and allows the user to make corrections within the document regardless of the original processor used. MegaDots works with voice, refreshable Braille, and large-print applications.[3]

The Screen-Reader Choice

Braille output has both a hardware and a software component. So far, much attention has been given to the hardware and software that produces

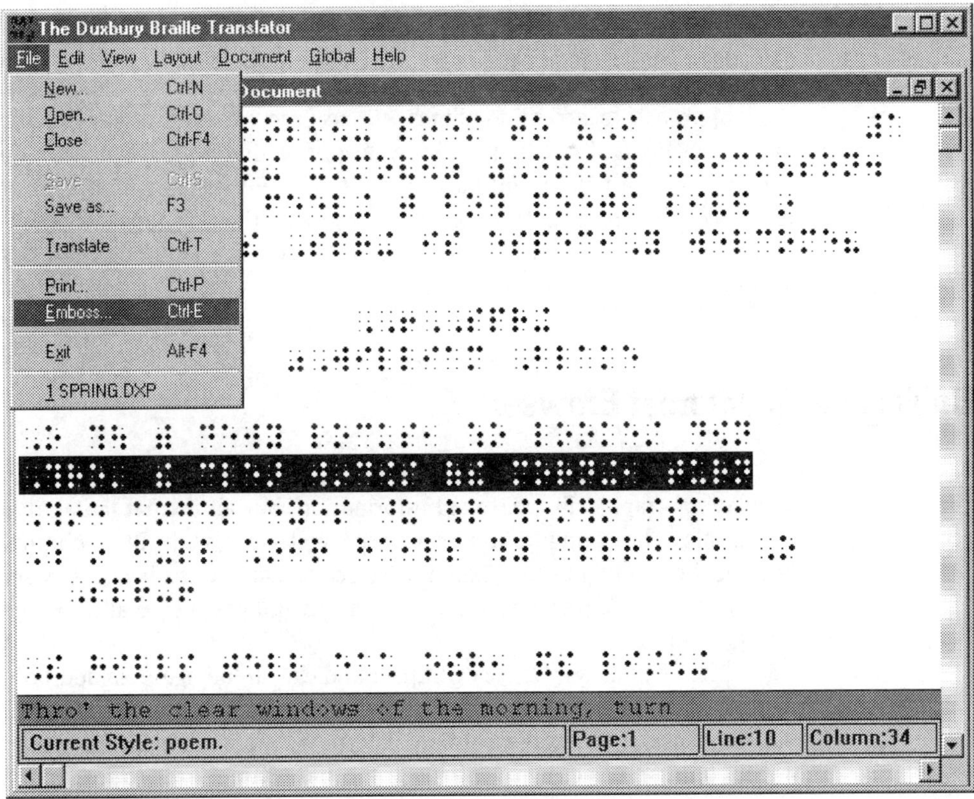

FIGURE 5-5
The Duxbury Braille Translator follows an easy-to-use menu system

the Braille output. For the display to function, however, a screen-reader software program must be running and sending information to the Braille display.

To some extent, the particular Braille display purchase will dictate what software should be purchased. Certain Braille displays will only work with the Braille display manufacturer's software. Other manufacturers have made their displays compatible with a variety of screen readers and will offer the library a choice about what to purchase. Probably the most important considerations will be what a library's patrons are using and the quality of local support from the vendor.

Integration of Speech and Braille

Speech-synthesizer systems provide another method for accessing computer information. The decision to install speech or Braille access is not an either-or question. First, a computer system can have both speech and Braille access installed, and it is possible for a patron to run the access of choice. Second, it is also possible to have speech and Braille access working together. When a coordination of speech and Braille output exists, the user has the opportunity to receive information tactually and audibly. This approach to access combines the accuracy of Braille reading (the user "sees" what is written) and the ease of having a program speak up when there is an important message. Often, Braille users will miss error messages that flash quickly on the screen and then disappear. Speech-output systems speak the message once it appears, whether or not it has disappeared from the screen.

Braille and the Internet Browser

No speech- or Braille-access configuration will be capable of directly displaying graphically presented information, but all textual material is accessible. The configurations discussed will work with all traditional Internet browsers (Internet Explorer, Netscape, etc.). A text-based browser called Lynx, however, can offer certain advantages, especially for the Braille user.

The Lynx display is very compact and easy to navigate. In addition, Lynx 2.5 and later versions support a special switch that was introduced for blind users. When the parameter "-show_cursor" is included on the Lynx Command line, Lynx will force the hardware cursor to follow the active link on the page. Thus, the Braille display will always show the text that is highlighted by the cursor.

Lynx: Tips to Enhance Braille Accessibility

Starting Lynx

Lynx is usually started by entering the Lynx command. The default Lynx page for the system will be displayed. For those using speech or Braille access, it can be very helpful to start Lynx with the show-cursor switch. Enter "lynx-show_cursor." This optional switch will force the system cursor to follow the currently selected link. The show-cursor option is not available on all systems.

The Lynx Display

All Lynx screens have a number of features in common that can be used for orientation. From top to bottom, these include:

1. The top line of each screen is the title of the page, if there is one.
2. In the top right corner of each screen is a Status line that tells the user how much of the document has been viewed. It is presented "(pg x of y)" with x the number of the screen presently being viewed and y the total number of screens on the page.

3. Lines 2 to 21 present the text of the page being viewed. The Active link is displayed as highlighted text for easy identification. All other links that may appear on the screen are displayed in boldface to distinguish them from the highlighted link and also from the surrounding text.
4. Line 22 often says "—Press space for next page—."
5. Lines 23 and 24 are usually a two-line menu, such as:

   Arrows: Up and Down to move. Right to follow a link; Left to go back.

   or

   H)elp O)ptions P)rint G)o M)ain screen Q)uit /= search
6. The g command allows any URL to be viewed. Pressing the g command will bring up a prompt asking for a URL. Type in the URL that you wish to view. The Up arrow will recall previously entered locations.

Lynx Searching Commands

While viewing a document, use the / command to find a word or phrase within the current document. You will be prompted with "Enter a whereis query:". Type the characters you wish to find and press <ENTER>. To find the same characters again, use <n>. The Up arrow will recall previous search queries.

Lynx Options Menu

The Lynx Options Menu may be accessed by pressing <o> . These options can be helpful in improving accessibility:

Keypad serves as arrows or numbered links. This option gives the choice between navigating with the arrow keys or having every link numbered so that the links may be selected by numbers as well as by using the arrow keys. Numbered links can be very useful for speech and Braille users because selecting a link directly by number avoids the necessity of cursoring up or down to select the desired link.

The User mode offers three possible operating choices: Novice, Intermediate, and Advanced. In the Novice mode two lines of Help are displayed at the bottom of the screen. The Intermediate mode turns off the Help lines, while the Advanced mode displays the URL of the currently selected link at the bottom of the screen.

Other Items to Aid Braille Users

Keytops

It is possible to purchase Braille/large-print overlay keytops for a standard keyboard. These are simply applied over the keys and offer the user a tactile reminder of which keys his or her fingers are touching. While some Braille readers scoff at the need for the tactile keys, others who never learned to use the keyboard do need them. These keytops are available from Hooleon Corporation.[4]

Location of Workstation a Consideration

If possible, locate the Braille workstation near the standard workstations. Many times well-meaning managers will locate the accessible workstation in areas that offer more privacy to the user; this means, however, that the patron will have to take a path that may be laden with obstacles. If there is no alternative to the location of the workstation, alert the staff to remove trucks and inform the patron of items that may in a pathway.

Braille Access—a Rewarding Challenge

Providing Braille access to the Internet may seen daunting because it is specialized and expensive, but it is well worth the challenge. While speech synthesizers yield the text presented, Braille displays are the only facility to give the user information on how the screen appears, with the exception of graphics (which are still presented as "islands").[5]

Notes

1. For further information concerning the history and use of Braille, visit the Websites of the International Braille Research Center at <www.braille.org>; Introduction to Braille and Braille Transcribing at <www.shodor.org/braille>; and the New York Institute for Special Education History of Reading Codes for the Blind at <www.nyise.org/blind/barbier.htm>.
2. Visit the Duxbury Website at <www.duxburysystems.com>.
3. For more information on MegaDots, contact Duxbury Systems at <www.duxburysystems.com>. Duxbury also maintains a useful Website for Braille access issues.
4. Contact Hooleon directly at Hooleon Corporation, 411 South 6th Street, Building B, Cottonwood, AZ 86326; or phone (520) 634-4503 or (800) 937-1337; or visit their Website at <www.hooleon.com>.
5. Stig Becker et al., "CESAR Comparative Evaluation of Screen Alternatives for Reading," *Closing the Gap* (June/July 1997): 3. DBT will work with applications such as voice output and refreshable Braille.

6 Adaptive Technology for Hearing Impairments

Many people have hearing disabilities yet are not considered deaf. These hearing impaired people may have difficulty distinguishing audio output from background noise, but they can hear satisfactorily if the distraction is removed; or they may be able to hear male voices but not female voices; or they may be able to hear if the sounds are amplified. Many times all that is needed by people with hearing impairments is a set of computer headphones and the ability to increase the output's sound level. Persons who are deaf, however, cannot hear at all; they rely on visual skills for communication (such as ASL or lip-reading).

Making Sounds Visual

Because access to computers is basically a visual process, persons with hearing disabilities rarely encounter serious barriers when interacting with software. When sound is used to indicate a user action, however, alternate visual data must accompany the sound. For instance, a printer emitting a beep when it is ready to print is not a sufficient cue to the user who is deaf; it is necessary for the user to receive a visual cue.

Software Solutions

SoundSentry and Show Sounds are two sound-property adaptions provided by Microsoft as part of its Windows Accessibility Options package. The activation is extremely easy to use. Activation is achieved simply by choosing the alerting options you desire, such as Flashing Active Caption Bar, Flashing Active Window, or Flash Desktop. The screen will respond accordingly when sounds are found as part of the output. Show Sounds is a sound-property adaption that provides text captions within Microsoft utilities where sound is used.

SeeBeep for Windows, available for a nominal shareware fee from Microsystems Software, will work with Windows 3.x, Windows 95, and MS-DOS. SeeBeep is one of the original computer adaptions designed for persons with hearing impairments. Activating SeeBeep will prompt a flash screen in reverse video or present a visual beep bitmap on-screen each time the computer makes a sound. A demonstration is available on Microsystem's Website.[1]

Telecommunications Devices

In addition to computer adaptions to help the hearing impaired, other devices are available to aid persons with oral communication disabilities. Both the hearing and speech impaired can benefit greatly from the telecommunication devices that are currently available.

Once you understand the concept of Teletypewriters (TTYs), you understand that the TTYs' very operating style is the foundation for e-mail and chat rooms. The communications provision of the ADA Title IV mandated that the telephone companies provide a relay service for persons who are hearing or speech impaired. This is a very difficult and inefficient way to provide service. The person who has a TTY (sometimes called a Telecommunication Device for the Deaf (TDD)) types a message to an operator who reads the message to the person being called; that person then relays the reply to the operator who types it back to the TTY user! While the relay operators are trained to echo the message verbatim, there is still the chance of losing keywords. This process is also very time-consuming.

A TTY should be installed at your reference desk and in your public phone area. Basically, a TTY is a special device that is used by a hearing impaired person, deaf user, or a speech impaired individual to type a message to either an impaired or nonimpaired user. The typed message goes through a phone line and appears in the viewing window of the other TTY. The hearing impaired user is signaled that the phone is ringing by a flashing light on the phone (many home users have remote signaling flashers as well so they do not have to watch a phone); nonimpaired users prefer to interface the unit with an inexpensive phone to hear the ring. The TTY is extremely easy to set up; simply plug the phone jack into the wall jack and it is ready to make and receive calls. Reading the instruction book provided with each model will be sufficient to learn how to use the TTY.

The system that uses state-of-the-art electronics (these phones can be used to make overseas calls as well as local ones) is fast and reliable. Users are able to send their sentences as quickly as a person speaking on a conventional phone. Typical abbreviations include the following terms that are logical, making them easy to learn:

TTY ABBREVIATIONS

GA	—	Go Ahead (I'm finished typing, your turn)
SK	—	Stop Key (Conversation over, hang up)
CUZ	—	Because
HD	—	Hold, Please
PLS	—	Please
OIC	—	Oh, I See
U	—	You
UR	—	Your
CD	—	Could
Q	—	Question Mark
R	—	Are
NBR	—	Number
SHD	—	Should
TMW	—	Tomorrow

You will note that many of the abbreviations are the same as the ones used to quickly dash off e-mail messages.

Popular TTYs for Business Use

Krown Manufacturing

Krown Manufacturing was one of the very first companies to manufacture TDDs and is one of the industry leaders. Krown presently makes 13 models in its line (see figure 6-1 for an example), including two public payphone models. The more popular models include the Portaview PV20D, Portaview PV20+, Memory Printer MP20, Memory Printer MP20D, and Memory Printer MP40. The display is 20 characters in length. Portaview PV20D also has a 20-character readout but has a built-in printer that uses 2¼-inch thermal paper to record conversations; Portaview PV20+ has the same capabilities as the PV20D model, but also has Auto Answer capabilities. The Memory Printers series offers the same features as the Portaviews with the added advantage of having the capability of storing messages and phone numbers in the memory.

The Krown TTYs also have ASCII models that allow interfaces with computers. This naturally expands the possibility of communication and information exchange. More information can be obtained on Krown's products by visiting its Website.[2]

UltraTec Products

The UltraTec product line includes models of TDDs that print and those that don't and those that can interface with personal computers. Popular models, which include the Miniprint II, Superprint 4425, and Superprint

FIGURE 6-1
Krown TTY/TDD with printer

4225, are reasonably priced. All of the units are portable and work with a battery pack or standard electrical socket.

The Superprint 4425 is the deluxe version of a TDD and has a built-in 24-character printer, 32K memory, an auto-answering feature, and direct-connect keyboard dialing. Key features of the 4425 are that it is available with ASCII installed and a built-in "sticky key feature."

The user has a choice of three font display sizes that make the unit useful for persons with vision loss. The display window can display 20 characters at one time, making the print feature desirable (it also saves the user from having to take notes as the conversation progresses).

Additionally, UltraTec produces TTYs for public usage and has one model, the Uniphone, that serves as both a standard phone and a TTY. UltraTec maintains an excellent Website with detailed information on TTYs in general, product information, and Web links.[3]

Captioning the Sounds—I Need to See What You Are Saying

Using the software currently available, disabled persons now can experience full computer access, particularly through captioning, transcription of audio speech on Websites, and through other multimedia tools.

CAP-Media Tools

CAP-Media, Inc., has developed software that gives the user the facility to caption, annotate, and analyze computer media. The product, CAP-Media Tools, provides the user with templates to create interactive media presentations for the World Wide Web (Asymetrix's Neuron, a plug-in application for Web browsers, must be used in conjunction with CAP-Media).[4] Those who use the tools, home pages, and Websites are free to be creative with sound and visuals, for persons with disabilities will not be barred from full access.

Modifications include visual representation of audio for people who are deaf or hard-of-hearing and edited language representations of media for those with cognitive disabilities. Also, CAP-Media tools allow ASL and the text to be presented simultaneously. This also allows the user to present the audio in one language and subtitle the presentation in another.

QuickTime Video Clips

The CPB/WGBH NCAM has been experimenting with various methods to add captioning to Websites by using QuickTime video clips.[5] Thus far, they have been able to add captions to the text track (in addition to the audio and video track); this development will help in the presentation of online instructions. To receive a demonstration of the process, check out NCAM's Website.

Virtual Meetings

Currently, only a few roadblocks for the deaf exist on the information highway. This probably will change with the integration of computers, phones, and video. But with roadblocks also come the outer-belts, which take you around the traffic and deposit you where you want to be.

NetMeeting

With the introduction of NetMeeting, Microsoft has developed a product that stands to change the format of meetings. NetMeeting allows real-time text communication, the ability to form a corporate or scholarly "intranet" that allows off-site users to "meet" in virtual time and space. The advantages are many: People who are hearing impaired can participate fully, no travel time and expenses are involved, and the session can be saved as text (eliminating the need to process notes from the meeting).

The real-time voice-communication feature allows the user to enhance the text presentation with voice and provides an Electronic Whiteboard that allows sharing premade graphics and the creation of new graphics in real time. While the addition of graphics may hinder the user who is blind, the real-time voice feature will allow sighted users to describe the presentation. NetMeeting, a core component of Internet Explorer 4.0, will be incorporated into future releases of the Windows operating system and can be downloaded from the NetMeeting Website.[6]

I. King Jordan, president of Gallaudet University, Washington, D.C., the premier university for undergraduates who are deaf or hard-of-hearing (or students wishing a career in services to the deaf community), applauded Microsoft for this development. Jordan stated that "Gallaudet

University is committed to ensuring its students have the world's best interactive visual learning environment" and felt that "products like Encarta '98 and NetMeeting help ensure full and independent access to information and communication networks that deaf and hard-of-hearing people need to achieve their academic and life goals."[7]

Other Technologies for Hearing Impairments

Although persons with hearing impairments do not encounter many obstacles when accessing the Internet, they may face problems when instructions are verbally communicated. In addition to providing clearly written instructions for this group of users, adaptive devices should be acquired that will facilitate communication.

Easy Listener

The acquisition of a device called the Easy Listener allows a staff member to speak in a normal voice to a patron with a hearing impairment. The Easy Listener utilizes two components: a microphone transmitter that is worn by the speaker and a receiver that is worn by the listener. The microphone transmits the speaker's voice by an FM radio signal to the receiver worn by the listener (see figure 6-2). The loudness of the speaker's voice is adjusted by a volume control similar to that on a transistor radio. The loudness and clarity of the speaker's voice will not be affected by distance, so the listener may sit anywhere he or she chooses. All the user has to do is: (1) put the headset on; (2) turn the unit on and wait for the speaker to begin; and (3) when speaking begins adjust the volume control.

The Easy Listener is produced by Phonic Ear. More information about assistive-listening devices, as well as other information on communication aids, may be found on Phonic Ear's Website.[8]

FIGURE 6-2
The Easy Listener facilitates communication for persons with hearing impairments

Other assistive-listening devices are available in the marketplace. These devices are not always advertised as "hearing assistants" but rather as eavesdropping tools. They are available at electronic stores and through technology catalogs and will serve to aid communication.

Infrared Transmission

Another kind of technology that helps people who are hearing impaired fully enjoy the library facility is infrared transmission. An infrared emitter is installed in a room and connected to the normal house sound system (see figure 6-3). People who need sound amplification wear headphones and receive an undistorted, amplified presentation of the speaker. More information on infrared transmission may be found at the Website of Phonic Ear, the producer of many infrared systems.

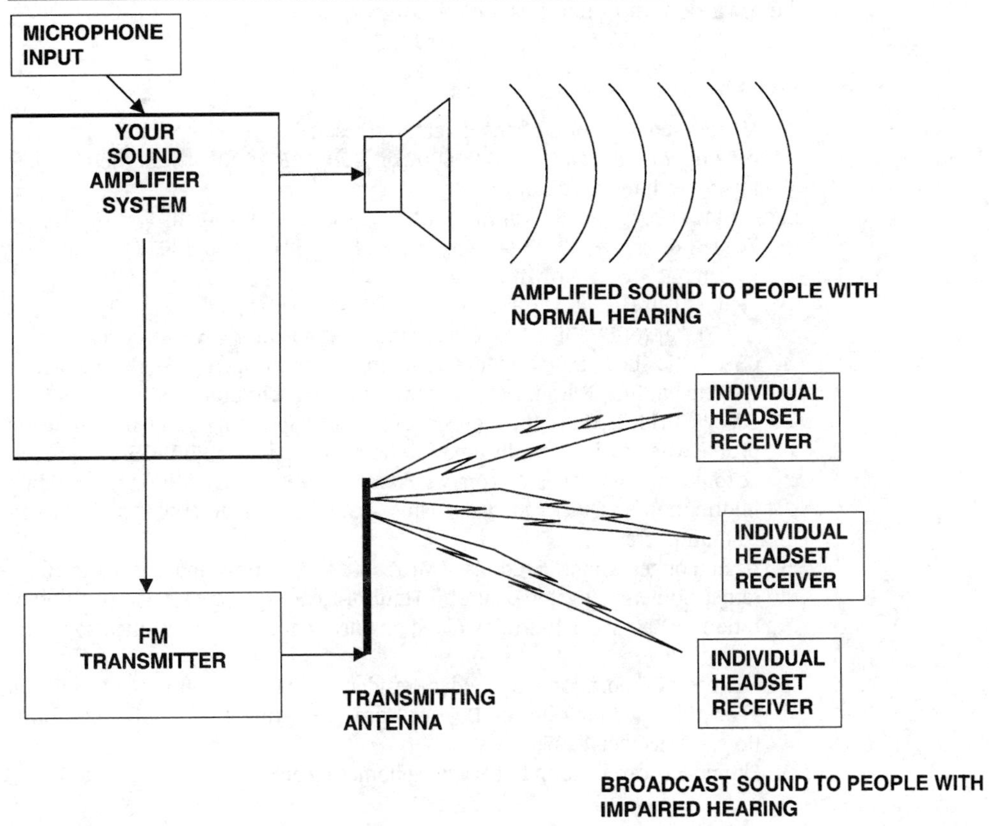

FIGURE 6-3
Use of local FM transmitter will allow all to hear the presentation

Signaling Devices

Visual displays are now standard additions to fire alarms and flash whenever the siren is discharged; remember, however, if only "voice" announcements to alert users to closings and special services are made, not everyone will be reached. A method must be in place so that everyone will "hear" the announcement—this may be a low-tech solution such as blinking the lights.

Low-Tech Solutions

Remember when looking for service solutions for the deaf and hard-of-hearing, the answers may be simple and on hand. For instance, if it is difficult to get a point across because a patron cannot understand speech, consider using a word processor as a slate in which the conversation is typed instead of spoken. Also keep a stack of message cards to use if vocal communication is not possible. Most of the time, these efforts will be rewarded and mistakes will be forgiven.

Notes

1. Microsystems is one of the original accessibility providers, with a trusted consumer base. Call (508) 875-8009 or (800) 828-2600; or visit their Website at <www.handiware.com>.
2. Contact Krown at: Krown Mfg., Inc., 3115 Lankland Road, Fort Worth, TX 76116; or call (817) 738-2485; or by TTY at (817) 738-8993; or visit their Website at <www.krowntty.com>.
3. Contact UltraTec at: UltraTec, Inc., 250 Science Drive, Madison, WI 53711; or call TTY at (608) 238-5400; or visit their Website at <www.ultratec.com>.
4. CAP-Media Tools, Software for Captioning, Annotating, and Analyzing Media, CAP-Media, Inc., Felton, Del., <www.cap-media.com/products>.
5. CPB/WGBH NCAM are the pioneers of "closed-captioning of media," allowing people who are deaf to fully enjoy audio presentations. CPB/WGBH NCAM can be found at <www.boston.com/wgbh/pages/access>. In addition to providing information on QuickTime video clips, many links on accessibility issues can be found here.
6. Dean Conger and Nik Corbis, "Microsoft NetMeeting and the Role of Internet Conferencing for Deaf and Hard-of-Hearing Users." Microsoft Corporation, 1998. Website to download NetMeeting is at <www.microsoft.com/msdownload>.
7. Microsoft Corporation, "Gallaudet President Visits Microsoft to View Products That Aid Students Who Are Deaf or Hard-of-Hearing." Microsoft, "Legal Notices," December 1997.
8. Phonic Ear can be found at <www.phonicear.com>.

7

Surfing the Internet with a "Different" Board

Access problems to computers by persons with physical disabilities are often caused by their inability to manipulate a standard keyboard. These individuals for this discussion are at least of average intelligence but are unable to move about and interact independently without assistive devices. Their physical disability can be congenital in nature, or caused by accidents resulting in spinal-cord injuries, vascular accidents that cause strokes, or diseases that cause loss of limbs or nerve degeneration.

While it does not seem as though it takes a great amount of coordination to simultaneously press <CONTROL>, <ALT>, and <DEL> to reboot a computer, for a person who lacks the ability to use both hands it is almost impossible. For most of us, pressing one key at time on a standard keyboard to input data is more a mental process than a physical process; for persons without the ability to totally control their hands, however, this is physically challenging. Adaptive hardware and software devices can help persons with physical disabilities access computers. Computer input devices allow persons who have control of a single muscle (a toe, a finger, an eye) to communicate and exchange information.

Some of these devices are highly specialized and will be of use to extremely small populations of persons with specific and varying degrees of disability. While it is not feasible to purchase every conceivable type of alternative input device, one should be aware of the items that are available and purchase those that are more mainstream in nature.

People with learning disabilities face a different set of access problems. Some persons with learning disabilities find it impossible to follow the Click Here command found on a busy computer screen, or enter keystrokes in the needed order. These people are at the very least of average intelligence, their vision is good, and their hands and fingers are fully functional, yet an impairment exists that makes it impossible for them to "see" the screen or use a standard keyboard. If presented with another type of input device, many individuals are able to seek and find information.

Voice Recognition for Both Learning Disabilities and Physical Impairments

Also known as speech recognition, this technology is simultaneously becoming more sophisticated and less costly with each product generation. David Arnold, of Olive Tree Software, stated that "speech recognition technology has changed a great deal every two years since 1990 . . . as computer power has altered what can be attempted."[1] Both Arnold and Michael Dertouzas, director of MIT's computer-science lab, predict that "speech will eventually replace the need to use the mouse and keyboard" and probably be used to offer "hands-free access to the computer when driving."[2]

Currently, however, voice recognition is a technology that allows a person to use his or her voice as an input device for computer commands. Voice recognition may be used to dictate text, World Wide Web addresses, or commands to the computer (such as saving documents or pulling items off a menu). Voice recognition uses a neural net to "learn" to recognize a person's voice. As the person speaks, the voice-recognition software remembers the way each word is pronounced. The computer will learn the nuances of the speech patterns by listening to the phonemes and committing them to memory.

This process requires the user to read aloud to the computer an excerpt from one of three books that are presented bit by bit on the computer screen for approximately 30 minutes. The software accuracy improves as it is used, and much like someone learning a new vocabulary, may mispronounce words until corrected. It takes a few days before the system yields a 95 percent accuracy rate in the reading, which may present a problem in the library environment, but the time periods do not have to be consecutive.

There are critics who claim that persons with learning disabilities are not aided by speech recognition access, yet others strongly maintain that for now this process of dictating words as input is the only way to instill students with good oral language skills. The advantage for both groups of users is the same: All they need to do is speak their desires to the computer rather than type the commands—a task that is difficult for different reasons. What may cause problems, however, is the need for patience in teaching the software speech patterns.

Three major speech-recognition vendors exist, as well as new vendors searching for a piece of this lucrative marketplace. The two that are the most familiar, IBM and Kurzweil, are relative newcomers to the technology, but the third, Dragon Systems, has been working for 20 years to develop speech-recognition software.

Evaluators found that the products are extremely similar, with the price well under $200. Experts offer basic tips for success with all the products:[3]

Basic Techniques for Increased Success with Speech Recognition

1. Consistent and correct microphone positions are the most important factors for success.
2. Consistent volume of speech is also important. If an intonation changes during the day, a second computer training session will be necessary.
3. Speak as naturally as possible. Many people may become self-conscious when speaking to the computer and say words in unaccustomed ways that they cannot repeat.
4. Speak clearly and say every part of the word rather than slurring or leaving off part of the word.
5. Speak at a consistent pace. Do not speak familiar words faster than those being said for the first time.

The Three Voice-Recognition Systems Compared

Dragon Systems

Dragon Naturally Speaking Preferred will work in the Windows and Windows NT environment. Product developers claim that the product can input 160 words per minute, but product evaluators were unable to speak at a rate faster than 100, which the product was able to handle.[4] The Dragon product lets the user verbally select misinterpreted words and spell out the corrections; for example, if he or she says, "Find me a review of the book *Horse Whisperer*," and the computer thinks the user said "Horse with Spurs," he or she would simply say "select with Spurs" and repeat the correct word "Whisperer." The drawback of the product, obviously, is that it is a memory hog.

A team of researchers from the *Plain Dealer* tested the product by having it "listen and record" the first sentence of the Gettysburg Address. What they said was: "Four score and seven years ago comma our fathers brought forth upon this continent a new nation comma conceived in liberty and dedicated to the proposition that all men are created equal period."

The researchers dictated the sentence at a normal rate of speed. According to the results, Dragon Naturally Speaking made one mistake. It wrote "For" instead of "Four."[5]

IBM ViaVoice

The IBM ViaVoice program was not necessarily developed to be a speech-recognition product, but rather to integrate it into other applications such as Web browsers.[6] Additionally, it has licensed its speech engine to software makers and hopes to have it become a virtual assistant in the workplace. Although the company has greater aspirations for the product, the program still serves as a good speech-recognition system for accessing today's computers.

There is a learning period for ViaVoice and it is suggested that the user spend periods of 10 to 30 minutes with the program. If the user is willing to accept mistakes, he or she can skip this step. This may be a huge mistake, however, for correcting misinterpreted words is not an easy task and often needs the keyboard to facilitate the process.

When tested by the *Plain Dealer* using the Gettysburg Address (as previously mentioned and in endnote 5), IBM's ViaVoice made one mistake: It heard the word "on" instead of "upon."

Again, the price that needs to be paid for the product is memory. The product works with Windows NT as well as other Windows products.

Kurzweil VoicePlus

Kurzweil has long been a leader in adaptive products, having invented the first "computer reading" machine before most people knew what computers were. The corporation Alpha Software has developed an extremely economical program that does not require as much memory as either the ViaVoice or Dragon Naturally Speaking Preferred.

The current product does require the speaker to briefly pause between words, which is a problem if the user has difficulty focusing and keeping his or her train of thought.

When tested by the *Plain Dealer* (as previously mentioned and in endnote 5), the speech-recognition program made two mistakes: It typed a numeric "4" rather than wrote the word "four" and heard the word "vacated" instead of the word "dedicated."

Voice Power for Windows

Voice Power for Windows is one of the new products that has been tested by the University of Toronto Adaptive Technology Resource Center and found to work successfully in Windows applications for persons with disabilities.[7]

This is an off-the-shelf product, available anywhere software is sold. It advertises itself as being a totally "Hands Free" control of Windows 95 and NT, with the ability to launch any Windows application by Voice, including Netscape and Explorer.

Physical Disabilities May Require Software Adaptions to the Standard Keyboard

As stated previously, disabilities that prohibit physically handicapped persons from accessing computers are varied. Some people's only physical disability is the inability to access more than one side or one key of the computer at a time, which inhibits them from using an application program that calls for the user to press <CTRL> and <ENTER> to define a hard page. These software programs also help alleviate key repeats when a key is held down too long by a person who may not be able to move his or her hands quickly from the keys or may be using a mouthstick or headstick to push the keys down.

Microsoft's Accessibility Tools

Microsoft Corporation added several features to Windows 95 and Internet Explorer that make it easier for persons with physical impairments to access information. These include:

- "StickyKeys" simulate the simultaneous pressing of the <SHIFT>, <CTRL>, and <ALT>. The user presses the <SHIFT> five times to access the program and then is able to enter keystrokes sequentially that otherwise would have to be entered simultaneously.
- "FilterKeys" tells the Windows program to ignore brief or repeated keystrokes accidently activated by pressing a key too long. The user activates this feature by holding the right <SHIFT> for eight seconds. Settings can be adjusted.
- "ToggleKeys" when activated will signal the user with tones when <CAP LOCK>, <NUM LOCK>, or <SCROLL LOCK> is engaged or disengaged. This feature is activated by holding <NUM LOCK> for five seconds.
- "MouseKeys," an alternative for those lacking dexterity, allow the user to use the numeric keypad of the keyboard to move the mouse pointer. For instance, pressing </> will simulate the left mouse click, and pressing <+> is used to simulate a double click. This feature also allows the user to set the Top Speed and the Acceleration Speed.
- "Automatic Reset Turnoff" disables the Accessibility features after the features are idle for a user-set time period.
- "Serial Key Devices" allow alternative access to keyboard and mouse features. The user may adjust the baud rate of the Microsoft programs to coincide with the input device (such as a special keyboard).

Microsoft also points out that it has incorporated hundreds of keyboard shortcuts in its Explorer product, such as pressing <TAB> to allow easy navigation to move forward to hyperlinks and addresses or <SHIFT> and <TAB> to move backward to help persons with limited physical abilities. Other keyboard shortcuts can be found in the Internet Explorer Help Index, under Keyboard Shortcuts, or in the Microsoft Windows Keyboard Guide.

Experts who tested the modifications found that many of Microsoft's emulations were actually more reliable than those built into specialized keyboards.[8] When field-tested with persons with extreme physical limitations, the keyboard shortcuts were found to be quick and positive, and dramatically reduced input time. All the shortcuts, however, are not easy to learn or remember, for many are complicated. Additionally, some of the shortcuts did not function as the user perceived they would.

The list of the more frequently used shortcuts should be compiled into a readable list and placed at the workstation, *if* Microsoft products are in use. For other products, separate software packages and keyboards must be added for accommodation.

Shareware Products

1-Key

1-Key is a memory-resident program distributed by Regenesis Development Corporation. It was designed to allow the one-finger, headstick, or mouthstick computer user to use standard software and a standard keyboard (although input may be slow). Depressing and releasing one of the functions (i.e., <SHIFT>, <CONTROL>, or <ALT>) makes it active for the next key, allowing the user to sequence his or her commands. This program also allows the standard key-repeat function to be disabled (i.e., only one letter or symbol will type regardless of how long the key is held down).

One Finger

One Finger is distributed by the Trace Research Center and allows for "one-finger" (or mouthstick, or headstick) operation of the <SHIFT>, <CONTROL>, or <ALT>. The program is "smart" and automatically determines the type of keyboard and computer being used. It is easy to use—depressing and releasing one of the function keys makes it active turning on or off a program; depressing the key twice locks the key until it is unlocked. The program is memory-resident, but it can be manually turned off or on. The user can program the automatic repeat of the keys from 0.5 to 60 seconds and also program it to turn itself off.

Modifications for Standard Keyboards

A few adaptions can be purchased for approximately $50 that will allow a user with mobility impairments to use the standard computer keyboard. These users need the adaptions for various reasons: One patron may have poor muscle control, while another using a mouthstick may not be able to isolate the key he or she wants. While these devices will not allow the user to move through searches as quickly as one could with a special keyboard, they make access less frustrating.

FIGURE 7-1
Keyguards help locate the correct key

Keyguards

A keyguard (see figure 7-1) is a rigid template with holes positioned over each key. It helps the user to stabilize finger, hand, or stick movement and to select a key without accidently activating others. Keyguards help support the hand and allow the user to slide it across the keyboard without pressing any keys. Keyguards are removable and can be simply slipped (or taped, if necessary) over the keys when needed. Keyguards are extremely important when using a highly touch-sensitive keyboard.

Key Locks

KeyStoppers, a trademark of Hooleon, are different from keyguards, for they will disable specific keys that are deemed "hazardous" to the user who can use a standard keyboard, but who needs to be safeguarded from accidently hitting keys such as <EXIT> or <DELETE> through involuntary body motions. There are two types of KeyStoppers, "soft" and "hard." The soft KeyStopper will partially immobilize the key and require the user to exert more pressure to use it. The hard KeyStopper will prevent operation of the key altogether. These kits are easy to use—remove the keys with the key-pulling device, insert the soft or hard KeyStopper over the slot of the key stem, then replace the key, pushing firmly until it clicks. Key-locking devices should also be available through a PC manufacturer and from Hooleon. Note: If you have a patron who needs this modification, consider attaching to an inexpensive keyboard and switch the keyboard.

Disk Guides

While not part of the keyboards, disk guides allow the computer user with poor hand control to access computers more easily. The disk guide is positioned on a stable surface (unlike the "midway" up position of the A or B drives on most computers), allowing the user to steady his or her hand on the surface as he or she aligns the diskette with the drive opening. The guide attaches as easily as any added drives and is available as a replacement to both internal drives and external drives. The disk guide is priced at under $100.

Keyboards

Several different types of keyboards currently are available that enable the user with limited hand or wrist movement to access the computer for information. Typically, these patrons would be able to read the screen, but for some reason (arthritis, cerebral palsy, neurological damage) cannot physically type commands on a standard keyboard to give direction to the computer. There are simple ways to solve the keyboard-access problem and most are easily installed, are low cost (under $1,000), and will not cause the nonimpaired user problems if used as the keyboard at a standard workstation.

While it is commendable to purchase in anticipation of need it is not advisable as each patron with a keyboard modification need will need a different solution. You should, however, be aware of the varieties available.

Keyboards Are Available as Oversize Models and as Miniatures

Membrane keyboards can be used by patrons who do not have the physical ability to depress individual keys on a standard keyboard, and they also help the visually impaired persons who need a larger typeface key than commercial large-print keytops provide. The keys require various degrees of downward pressure to activate. Some will activate with half an ounce of pressure, enabling persons who have coordination but lack strength to activate them. Other keyboards require almost a pound of downward pressure for those who have strength but lack coordination (a key on a standard keyboard can be activated with about two ounces of downward pressure). These keyboards make it possible for a person who is able to hold a stick with some body part (i.e., mouth, little finger) to manipulate that stick to punch out commands and use the resources found on the computer, without accidently activating unwanted keys. These keyboards are similar to keypads found on some pocket calculators (i.e., flat with surface notations) and have a high-tech design that could thus serve as the keyboard in a shared disabled and abled workstation.

The membrane keyboards come in two sizes: "expanded" with large squares replacing keys and "small" with pocket calculator–size keys replacing the standard keyboard keys. The keyboard size depends on the needs of the user: An expanded keyboard would be needed by the individual who can target only large areas, and the miniature keyboards would be used by those with an extremely limited range of limb movement. The one element to look for when purchasing an adapted keyboard is built-in mouse simulation, a must for Internet access. Following is a list of keyboards that have been tested and found to support access.[9]

Expanded Membrane Keyboard

The Expanded Membrane Keyboard is a product of ComputAbility Corporation. These low-cost keyboards will work with Microsoft's serial interface accommodation. The keyboards, which require almost a pound of downward pressure to activate, are not so sensitive as standard keyboards, which is good for persons with poor dexterity or spastic muscles that cause them to regularly strike unwanted keys.

The key space for each of the 128 programmable keys measures 1.25 inches square and the keyboard's active area size is 20" × 10". The Expanded Membrane Keyboard can emulate the mouse cursor control, which can be controlled by a keystroke.

WinKing and PC Mini Windows Keyboard

WinKing and PC Mini Windows Keyboard are products of TASH Inc. They can be plugged directly into the keyboard port without requiring any additional hardware or software.

WinKing, as its name "King" indicates, is an oversize keyboard. The TASH PC Mini Windows Keyboard only requires a force of three and a half ounces to activate keys, which means they can be activated with a mouthstick, pointer, or fingers, and lets the user set the response time from zero to two seconds, so a user with a slow response time can linger on a key without its repeating. The WinKing keyboard also has an audio feedback feature that indicates when the key is pressed and when the information is sent to the computer, which, again, is helpful to the user who may not know if the pressure applied to the key activated a computer response. The keyboard also has a simultaneous "lighted latching" (e.g., <CONTROL>, <ALT>, <SHIFT>, and other functions) feature, which alerts the user if the functions are on or off.

The Unicorn Expanded Keyboards and Unicorn Mini

The Unicorn Expanded Keyboard II has become a standard in the adaptive-technology field. It has 128 large (1¼-inch square) user-definable keys, which can be grouped together as needed to form combinations such as <ALT-CONTROL-DEL>; these keys require the capability of exerting six ounces of downward pressure to activate. The large-size spaces are for the user who has either a visual disability or a coordination disability (there is a large target area). The inputting of the keyboard selection is easy for the novice, for helpful prompts walk the user through the keyboard selection. The keyboard is priced at under $500 and is available from a variety of sources.

If patrons do need the ability to enter data using a membrane keyboard, but do not necessarily need the ability to rearrange the keyboard, a model of the same keyboard is available that can be plugged directly into the keyboard jack and can be attached and detached quickly.

The Unicorn Mini keyboard is based on the same engineering principles as is the Unicorn Expanded Keyboard II. The Mini is designed for individuals with limited hand expansion or body movement (with coordination) who wish to access the personal computer. The individual need only exert three ounces of downward pressure to activate the keys. Like the Expanded, the Mini can be reprogrammed to move frequently used keys or key groupings to suit the user's needs. This keyboard measures 7½"× 4½"× ½" (basically the size of an adult hand). The Mini can be plugged directly into the keyboard jack, with no other type of installation needed.

Magic Wand Keyboards

In Touch Systems manufactures a line of miniature keyboards that require little physical strength to manipulate. The Magic Wand device (see figure 7-2) offers the user instant installation and access (no training needed) and offers full mouse and keyboard control at the same time. This is accomplished with dedicated mouse keys. This keyboard, while expensive, will work in all Internet environments and with minimal conflicts.

Input Devices beyond Keyboards

DARCI TOO

DARCI TOO is a unique device, which creates a seamless, transparent interface between the computer and a wide variety of alternate keyboard devices. This means that interface software between individual devices

FIGURE 7-2
Magic Wand—small size but maximum potential

is not needed. The DARCI TOO will enable users to use Morse code, scan mode, Darci code and matrix inputting access. This is a real plus for a computer station which will be used by more than one user, as individual software programs for each peripheral do not have to be installed. An optional program, Load and Store, will allow you to store set-up information for each individual who will access the computer with his or her individual access device.

Realizing that some people have multiple handicaps and that this may include vision loss in addition to the inability to physically use a standard keyboard, DARCI TOO will also control IBM's screen reader. In this mode, DARCI TOO replaces both the screen reader keypad and the keyboard, allowing the user a new level of computer control.

The DARCI TOO was designed to enable the computer novice to install it. All one needs to do is disconnect the computer's keyboard and mouse and connect DARCI TOO in their place. The keyboard is then reconnected along with any other type of control needed. The controls may include joysticks, switches, matrix keyboards, or other communications aids.

IntelliKeys

IntelliTools, Incorporated, designed IntelliKeys as a computer access solution for persons who have a wide variety of disabilities. The IntelliKeys keyboard is easy to install; all that is needed is a cable. The device plugs into the keyboard port of virtually any PC or Apple product. IntelliTools states that its keyboard will work with all software requiring a regular keyboard or mouse.

The keys are large and well spaced for good physical access by users with limited dexterity. They are designed using contrasting colors to enhance visual access.

This keyboard tolerates a wide variety of input devices, which will interface with a standard overlay, configured for input needs of the user. For those who cannot use one of the standard overlays, IntelliTools offers software, Overlay Maker, which will allow the creation of a specially designed overlay tailored to the user's needs.

The overlay is bar-coded and activated when placed on the IntelliKeys board. One of the standard overlays, for example, was designed for the user who cannot use a mouse; IntelliKeys comes with standard arrows, allowing the user to move the cursor in any direction. Another feature added for the user who cannot press two keys simultaneously is the capability to press them sequentially. This device allows the user to press the SHIFT key followed by a letter key to type a capital letter.

IntelliKeys also allows adjustment of the response to pressure on keys in a situation where a user may drag his or her fingers, activating unwanted symbols, as well as the ability to adjust the repeat rate for the user who cannot lift and move the fingers off the keys quickly.

This is helpful for patrons with arthritis and for those without physical disabilities who need to "think" with their hands on the keyboard.

Mouse Emulators

Certain individuals have disabilities that prevent them from using any type of keyboard. They may, however, be able to grasp items and manipulate them. With the need for mouse emulation, these devices have expanded. Some people use a trackball (see figure 7-3), sometimes called an upside-down mouse, for they are able to use a hand or foot to roll it and click its keys until their messages are input into the computer. Still others use pointing devices in conjunction with on-screen keyboards to enter data.

WinTrac

A product of MicroSpeed Inc., WinTrac emulates a mouse, but does not actually have to be moved (see figure 7-3). It has three buttons on it that when depressed will start the cursor moving; a motion-device driver monitors the rate at which the cursor is moved and adjusts the speed from 50 to 1,000 pulses per inch. This allows the person who is unable to lift his or her finger off the mouse button quickly to take his or her time, for the cursor is moving at the operator's speed, not at the standard keyboard speed. As its name (Win) indicates, it will work in the Windows environment.

Switches Used as Input Devices

Unlike previously discussed alternate methods of inputting information into the computer by persons unable to access the standard keyboard, switches are probably the most radically different format used to input information. Switches are used only by the most severely physically disabled. Switches, when used in conjunction with hardware or software devices, provide input to the computer that is identical to typing in

FIGURE 7-3
A trackball is a pointing device

the information using a conventional keyboard. The device "switches" the input language of the user to keyboard language that the computer recognizes.

Switches as Signaling Devices Need Morse Code or Scanning Devices

There are a wide variety of signaling devices or switches being marketed which, when interfaced with software programs such as Morse code or on-screen scanners, allow persons with severe physical limitations to access computers (see figure 7-4).

Morse code interface programs are available with various features; however, all require the user to learn and know Morse code. Several Morse code interfaces are available which will work with most switches.

HandiCode and HandiCode Plus

Available from Microsystems, HandiCode and HandiCode Plus are extensive Morse code input devices with total keyboard functionality using any type of switch. They have macro capability, which allows any series of key strokes to be combined. HandiCode will work with DECTalk and other synthesizers to allow voice output capabilities. Some users may attain input speeds of up to 99 words per minute. Both devices have a PracticeCode utility that helps the user gain experience in using Morse code.

EzMorse and ezMorse for Windows

Neil Squire Foundation offers EzMorse and ezMorse for Windows as shareware. The Windows program allows the user to access by Morse code all programs that run in a Windows environment. The user is able to set the parameters and change speed of entry. The shareware is available for downloading at the Neil Squire Foundation Website: <www.neilsquire.ca>.

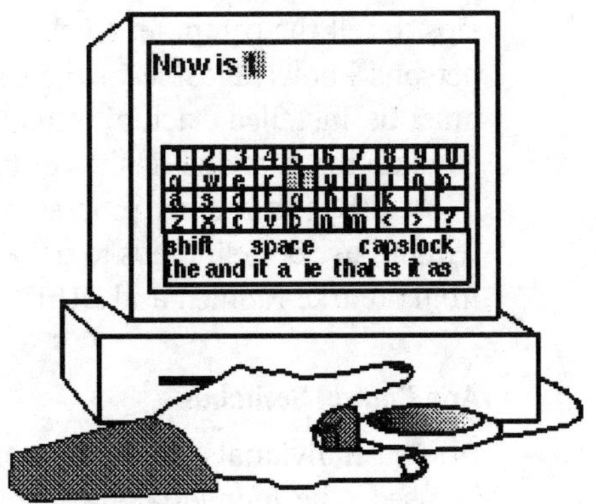

FIGURE 7-4
Using a switch to access

Scanning Devices

There are two types of scanning applications that, when interfaced with switches, can access computers and information: direct scanning, in which a user points to the target item using a single action, and indirect scanning, in which the cursor moves from one character to the next until it is at the spot where the user wants input made.

Switch Interface

The ramifications of switch interfacing go beyond information access. Features of dwellings as well as appliances can be configured to interface with a computer. This means lights can be turned on and off with the flick of a fingertip or the lift or the nod of a head. Computers and switches offer individuals who are quadraplegic the option of independent living.

Switches are placed within reach of the body part over which the individual user has voluntary control. For instance, if an individual only has voluntary use of a foot, he or she would be using a foot switch placed within reach of that foot. The same would be true if the person is using a chin switch. The connecting cord would be threaded through a device that would reach a mount for the switch, which would be within reach of the user's chin.

Mouth Control Using Sip-and-Puff Switches

Sip-and-puff switches are used by individuals to emulate the physical action of using the keyboard or mouse. Usually the individual who uses the sip-and-puff switch does not have consistent control of the hands to the degree of being able to accurately tap in commands on one of the alternate keyboards. He or she may rely on the ability to apply pressure (puffing) and suction (sipping) through disposable straws to dictate the direction the cursor will move. The switches may interface with either an on-screen keyboard or Morse code.

The individual using an on-screen keyboard moves the cursor by puffing until the cursor is on the desired letter or command, and then sips to tell the computer to choose the letter or command indicated. For persons knowledgeable in the use of Morse code (application software must be installed), actual letters may be entered using puff and sip to emulate the dots and dashes of the code.

Although a slow process, the sip-and-puff switch allows persons without use of their limbs to travel the world. These switches are available from Prentke-Romich and DU-IT.

Arm Control Switches

For the individuals with arm control, arm-control switching units can be used. The individual's arm rests in a cradle of slots, with each slot representing a different movement. The individual moves the arm from slot to slot to simulate the arrow keys of the keyboard. A slot also acts as the <ENTER> key. The arm-control switches must use a Morse code software or an on-screen keyboard display.

Head Control Switches

One notable switch manufacturer, Prentke-Romich, states that "if you can move your head, you can move the world" to encourage those who can move only their heads that they can access computers, technology, and life. There are switches, such as HeadMaster from Prentke-Romich, that resemble headphones. The device, which slips around the head, measures the rotation of the head; it then sends this measurement to the control unit that, in turn, signals the cursor to move. Selection is then made by a sip or a puff.

The Right Switch for the Need

Because such a wide variety of switches is available, there are "needs-assessment" professionals at the companies that produce switches (Prentke-Romich, TASH, CompuAide, ZYGO) who are able to determine the right type of switch to be used by the impaired individual by conducting a battery of tests. It is highly unlikely that one specific switching configuration will be used by more than one person in your community. In fact, the reason so many types of switching devices are available today is because some severely physically impaired individual somewhere needed an entry point to communication and someone capable of designing it did so and made it available to others. Persons using switches may know what switches they can use and bring the switching device with them, if they know that the library will provide a computer with an adaptive serial interface, such as DARCI, a port(s), and software that can be used with the switch.

While it is impossible to purchase switches in anticipation of need, an interface card or software purchased and installed in the computer will allow access and growth of switch applications. Most are highly versatile and capable of multiple functions (i.e., will serve as the interface for a membrane keyboard and a switch).

On-Screen Keyboards for Severe Physical Impairments

On-screen keyboards allow persons using switches, trackballs, or mouse emulators to use computers and the Internet. Several on-screen keyboard packages, such as the one offered by WiViK (see figure 7-5), allow access to Windows-based programs by users who are using a variety of switches to access the computer.[10]

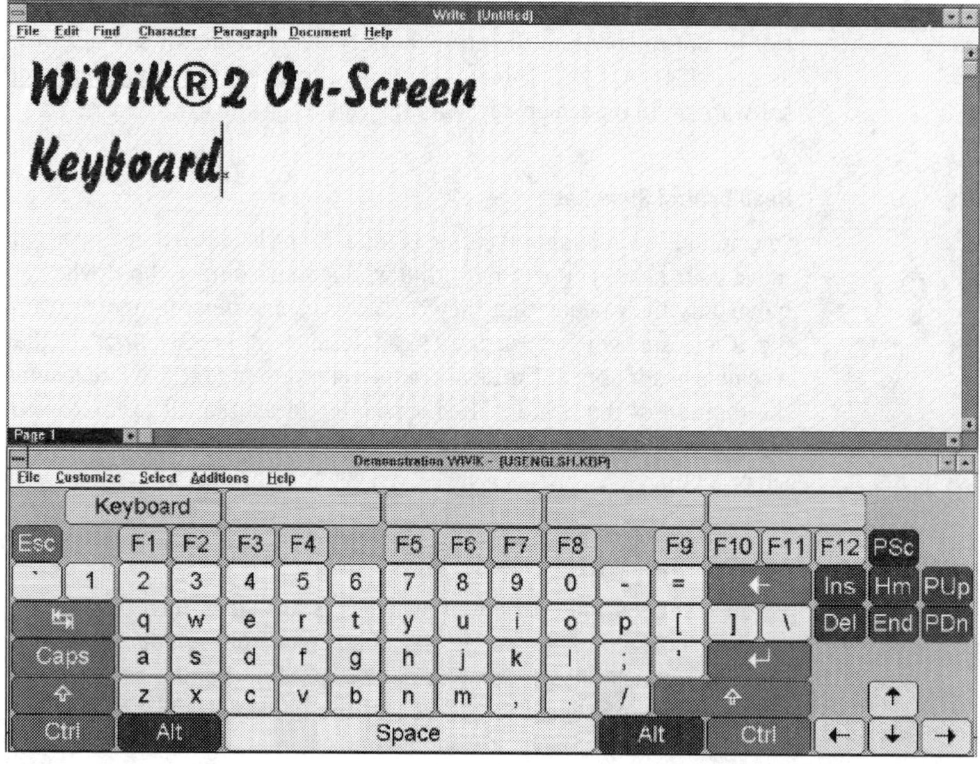

FIGURE 7-5
On-screen keyboard allows users to point to the keys rather than press them

WiViK

WiViK, in fact, will allow the user to add up to five switches and still maintain access to the printer. The individual may even use Morse code if needed to signal input. The individual moves the cursor by puffing until it reaches the key he or she wants to input and then sipping to tell the computer that this letter is his or her choice. Varying degrees of pressure are needed to activate the devices; however, all need some type of interface (either hardware or software) to alert the computer to look for the "sips" and "puffs" and recognize them as keyboard functions.

This device also can be used by someone using a "head-pointer" to enter data. This input device, as its name indicates, is mounted on the head and allows the user to activate mouse commands by directing the on-screen keyboard and mouse with head tilts and turns.

WiViK also includes programs with speech output for letters, words, sentences, and menus that appear on Web pages, provided a sound card is available. Speech output is also available as a stand-alone.

Visual Surfboard

Visual Surfboard is a set of tools that, in addition to providing an on-screen keyboard, provides the user with an easier way to navigate Web browsers such as Netscape or Internet Explorer. By activating the Universal Dwell program, people who cannot use a mouse are still able to activate links in the browsers. All they need to do is pause a pointer over the desired target for a defined period of time and the program will generate the clicks to take them there. The Visual Surfboard program is a product of Adaptive Computer Systems, which will provide a demonstration version of the product.[11]

The Right Furniture

One extremely important and basic need is purchasing furniture designed for the physically handicapped. Keep in mind that the patron using a wheelchair to navigate the library and access the computer has to be able to "wheel" himself or herself under the table on which the computer rests; choose furniture that will allow this (adjustable-height tables allow for different-sized wheelchairs and users). Also be sure that the computer is at a comfortable viewing height; persons in wheelchairs spend a lot of their time looking up and anything that can be done to alleviate this is a plus.

Choose a sturdy, well-balanced chair that will not roll or tip for the workstation seating. Often a person using a wheelchair would like to transfer from the wheelchair to the workstation chair, and he or she needs to know that the transfer will be a safe one. A chair with arms (although not standard in a computer workstation) and four legs is a wise choice for people using walkers or canes, for it presents a stable base to transfer their weight.

Architectural accessibility is as important as technical accessibility. Selecting and planning for adaptive technology for persons who need alternate input devices to access computers is the most difficult problem to solve in a public library setting. Choosing the right furniture and locating the workstation in an accessible location is the logical first step. A logical second step would be to acquire and install voice-recognition software on one workstation that will help those who have the patience to learn the device's nuances. A hidden perk for voice recognition is that it offers opportunities for cross-cultural learning experiences for patrons without disabilities.

Third, explore adding trackballs and trackpads along with use of mouse keys before adding an accessible keyboard to one of the workstations; none of these items would cause problems for patrons without disabilities. Also rewrite directions for using Microsoft's Accessibility Tools and Keyboard Shortcuts; again, you may find users without disabilities accessing these "electronic curb cuts" for many do save keystrokes and time.

Finally, other adaptions do exist and patrons may need to use items such as switches in your library. The easiest solution to this situation is simply to ask all patrons what their actual needs are, assuring them that the library will try to accommodate those needs but also warning them that doing so simply may not be possible. This action is in keeping with the ADA.

Notes

1. David Arnold, "Speech Recognition—Applications and Limitations for Motor Impaired, Learning Disabled, and Speech Impaired Operators" (Maryland Heights, Mo.: Olive Tree Software, 1998). Speech delivered at the 1998 CSUN Conference sponsored by California State University, Northridge, Center on Disabilities, March 1998.
2. Brad Stone, "Are You Talking to Me?" *Newsweek,* March 2, 1998, pp. 85–86.
3. Arnold, "Speech Recognition," 5.
4. Ibid.
5. Chuck Melvin, "His Master's Voice: Software Now Makes It Possible to Tell Your PC Exactly What You Want," *Plain Dealer,* January 19, 1998, 5C. In the study, the 30 minutes was spent training the programs to recognize speech patterns. The sentence was read five times and the last reading was recorded.
6. Stone, "Are You Talking to Me?"
7. Lake Porter, "Voice Recognition System." Glossary of Adaptive Technologies: Voice Recognition (Toronto: University of Toronto, Adaptive Technology Resource Centre). Found at <www.utoronto.ca/atrc/tech/voicerecog>.
8. Alan Cantor, "Avoiding the Mousetrap: An Evaluation of Keyboard-Only Access to Windows." Paper presented at the 1998 CSUN Conference sponsored by California State University, Northridge, Center on Disabilities. Text available at <www.dinf. org/csun_98>.
9. Laurie McArthur, "Adaptive Technologies: Alternative Keyboard Systems," Technical Glossary (Toronto: University of Toronto: Adaptive Technology Resource Centre [ATRC], 1997). Available at <www.utoronto.ca/atrc>.
10. WiViK products are available from Prentke-Romich, 1022 Heyl Road, Wooster, Ohio 44691; <www.prentrom.com>.
11. To receive a demonstration copy of Visual Surfboard, visit the Website of Adaptive Computers at <www.adaptivecomputer.com>.

8

Computers Reading and Speaking—"Stand-Alone" Systems

Arkenstone, a manufacturer of optical character recognition (OCR) reading products, has as its motto, "The Dawn of a New Day in Reading." Its product line, as well as that of Kurzweil Educational Systems, Telesensory, and JBliss Imaging, offers much to persons with disabilities who cannot read standard text. These systems are unique and make reading and learning accessible to persons with learning disabilities, such as dyslexia, and people who are visually impaired or blind or have mobility impairments.

Unlike software and hardware enhancements that are added on to standard computers, these devices are stand-alone systems that can be used to access information found and printed from the Internet as well as read printed documents and bound books. The systems are based on inventor Raymond Kurzweil's original reading machine that, although a marvel in its time, was expensive and required dedicating a full-time assistant to training patrons in its use.

Today's systems cost a fraction of what they used to and the need for intensive training is almost nonexistent. The producers realized that although persons with learning disabilities and people who were visually impaired were both text impaired, their computer access needs could be different. Consequently, the producers developed computer systems that are geared to helping specific disability groups, in addition to a generic system that all persons who are text impaired can use. Be aware, however, that the attributes added are only marginally disability-specific and that one group of disabled users may not be able to use a computer system designed for another.

The manufacturers also added features that allow people to use the scanners in libraries and take the scanned material home on a diskette for use within their own computer environments.

Currently, the two big names in reading systems are Arkenstone and Kurzweil; however, other corporations such as Telesensory and JBliss

Imaging Systems are garnering part of the marketplace and still other companies are being incorporated. Futurists see that this technology, originally developed for persons with disabilities, may be used in international mainstream settings, for it facilitates communications and is a time-saver.

The devices function in very similar fashion and the brand chosen depends on dealers and location. The National Center for Learning Disabilities (NCLD) suggests that persons considering purchasing equipment always ask many questions about the product and request a demonstration or references of sites that are successfully using the devices.[1]

The Arkenstone's OCR Reading Device Product Line

An Open Book

An Open Book is the foundation of Arkenstone's reading product line. It (see figure 8-1) uses a scanner to take a picture of the page and send it to the PC, at which point the synthesizer will either read it aloud or store the text in a file to be read at a different time.

Commands are given to Open Book through a specialized keypad. While it takes a few training sessions to learn how to use Open Book, most users are not dissuaded and return to use the equipment. Cassette and diskette tutorials are included with the equipment, as is "a quick-start" guide that allows the novice to jump in and scan a document immediately.

An Open Book will read most commercial-size print and interprets a dozen languages. And the user can take the scanned information home on a diskette.

VERA

VERA, an acronym for Very Easy Reading Appliance, is one of Arkenstone's latest inventions. Designed for persons with visual impairments, it can be used by persons with learning disabilities as well. VERA offers the user two options: He or she can either hear the text that was scanned or see it

FIGURE 8-1
An Open Book

displayed on the screen in large print. The display options include some of the attributes of a CCTV, for the user can change the display colors.

VERA uses a keypad with large-print/tactile keys. The most useful feature of these keys, however, is that each serves only one function, making it unnecessary to learn complicated formulas to operate the device.

VERA's newest feature is the availability of a modem. The modem allows the user to easily gain Internet access and to listen to the text found online or view the text in a font size that he or she is able to see.

WYNN

WYNN, an acronym for What You Need Now, was designed for users who can physically see the screen but find reading it impossible. WYNN furnishes the user with easy-to-use tool bars that allow the individual to modify the page to suit his or her specific needs.

For instance, if the user finds that the text is too small or too crowded, WYNN can enlarge it and change the spacing between the lines or words. It will also allow the user to mask out portions of the page to see the remaining words more clearly.

Another tool that can be used is the synthesizer. The synthesizer can read word for word while the screen display highlights the words that are being read.

Items found on the Internet will have to be downloaded and scanned.

More information about all these devices can be found at Arkenstone's Website.[2]

Raymond Kurzweil's New Generation OCR Reading Device Line

Omni 3000

The Omni 3000 was developed specifically to help people with learning and reading disabilities improve their reading comprehension skills and learn to enjoy reading. Using OCR technology, the Omni 3000 provides an auditory and visual presentation of scanned text and images.

The device speaks and highlights text (it can also magnify individual words), providing the reader with both a visual and an auditory representation of what is being read. Omni 3000 gives the user a choice of several clear synthetic voices (these range from a child's voice to adult male and female readers) and the option to use the reader's own voice to give commands to the computer, for it is equipped to handle voice recognition.

To use the Omni 3000 for Internet access, documents from the Internet will have to be scanned and then read by the Omni 3000.

Kurzweil 3000

The Kurzweil 3000 is Raymond Kurzweil's latest technology offering. In addition to being able to duplicate all the features of the Omni 3000, the Kurzweil 3000 can access the Internet in real time. This new version will allow the user to download text information and have it scanned and read aloud.

Omni 1000

The Omni 1000 was specifically designed for the blind. It allows the user to issue commands, such as repeating text and increasing reading speed, via the Omni's keypad. One important feature of the Omni is that it offers two versions: "Quick," which scans and reads documents with single or multiple columns and vertical or horizontal text; and "Quick Plus," which has all the attributes of "Quick" but adds file-management and voice-recognition commands.

For the latest information about the Kurzweil line of OCR devices, visit its Website.[3]

The Telesensory OCR Reading Device Product Line

The OsCaR Scanning System

Telesensory uses the most-advanced recognition technology to allow the user to scan text and convert it to a usable medium. Internal sensors align the document and adjust scanning sensors to get the best possible scan. It reads document text as small as 6 points or as large as 72 points.

The Telesensory product can read and translate two languages simultaneously and offers the user a choice of 11 languages. These features are extremely helpful in certain areas that have large immigrant populations.

One advantage for users who are blind is that OsCaR will work the Telesensory product line and convert the text into Braille and display scanned text into large-print type. Items from the Internet will have to be downloaded and scanned.

The PowerReader Assistant

This device from Telesensory is a product that plugs into a PC's serial port and sound card. It has most of the attributes of the OsCaR system and is operated through a supplied control panel. The control panel has a built-in microphone that allows the user to orally name documents and a button for all other controls.

For more information about Telesensory's OCR line of "reading machines," visit the Telesensory Website.[4]

The JBliss Imaging Systems OCR Reading Device Line

VIPinfoSoft Reading System

VIP stands for Versatile Image Processor and is the creation of James Bliss, currently president of JBliss Imaging Systems (formerly president of TeleSensory). Bliss's goal when creating the VIP line was to totally exploit computers to aid persons with low vision to access information. Many attributes of the VIPinfoSoft Reading System will also aid learning-disabled patrons.

Like other scanning systems, the VIP system will convert documents into digital images and allow the user to choose the output format that will allow him or her to read. VIP offers options previously available only to CCTV users (adjusting background colors, adding more space between letters, one-line-at-a-time display, split-screen images).

The system also takes advantage of synthetic speech, for it synchronizes highlighted text with the text displayed on the screen. This feature makes it usable by persons who are learning disabled.

VIPinfoNet Internet Browser

Like the VIPinfoSoft System, the VIPinfoNet Browser was designed to allow low-vision people to access the Internet; it also can be used by persons with learning disabilities. VIPinfoNet electronically processes Web pages so readers can view them in their choice of three presentation modes and synchronize them with natural-sounding speech. The browser can be launched from the VIPinfoSoft program or run as a separate program. The product supports image zooming, Graphic Interchange Format (GIF) animation, and embedded-imaging narration. Additionally, the VIPinfoNet Browser allows users to see all links—a summary of page links, image links, and text links.

Audiocassette tutorials that lead the user through the setup and operation of the VIP systems and "Cheat Sheets" are available at a nominal cost. The tutorial kit includes locator dots to mark certain keys. For more information on JBliss's OCR scanners and product line, visit the Website.[5]

Are OCR Reading Systems the Answer to Access?

Does it seem like the OCR reading systems are for everyone? They very well may be. Currently, they do a fairly good job of translating plain text and each generation will improve the quality of the scan.

Three of the scanning systems mentioned offer direct access to the Internet. This development was very recent so the other competitors will surely follow suit with an Internet module.

As Internet access is increasingly facilitated through these reading machines, they will surely become the preferred adaptive technology even if they require an extra computer. Anytime you eliminate the need for third-party software, there is a greater chance for success.

Notes

1. The National Center for Learning Disabilities maintains a tollfree information and referral line at (888) 575-7373.
2. For more information on Arkenstone, contact Arkenstone, 555 Oakmead Parkway, Sunnyvale, CA 94086; or call (408) 245-5900 or (800) 444-4443; or visit their Website at <www.Arkenstone.org>.
3. For more information about Kurzweil, contact Kurzweil Educational Systems, 411 Waverly Oaks Road, Waltham, MA 02154; or call (800) 894-5374 or (617) 893-4157; or visit their Website at <www.kurzweiledu.com>.
4. For more information on Telesensory, contact Telesensory Products, 520 Alamanor Avenue, Sunnyvale, CA 94086; or call (800) 286-8484 or (408) 616-8700; or visit their Website at <www.telesensory.com>.
5. For more information on JBliss, contact JBliss Imaging Systems, P.O. Box 1746, Los Altos, CA 94023, or call (408) 246-5783; or visit their Website at <www.jbliss.com>.

9

Funding Adaptive Technology

While it is becoming increasingly difficult to find funds for special projects, it is possible and well worth the effort. Many guides are available on this subject, but simply put, "Funders need to find worthy recipients for their dollars." Organizations that follow three basic steps when applying for funding for assistive technology will have a slightly better chance at gaining success.[1]

Step 1: Define Your Needs

The grant's administrator should receive specific reasons why it is necessary to add adaptive technology to a library. The statement "So my entire community will be able to use the library" will not suffice. It is better to say, "Statistics indicate that approximately 2,000 young adults with a learning disability live in our community. For these young people, reading is a chore rather than a joy and doing research is intolerable. These students would be able to use the WYNN and Kurzweil 3000 units to independently access the Internet. The information found therein will help the students attain higher marks in school and build a solid educational foundation that will help them attain academic and professional success."

Adaptive technology is still very foreign to most of the population and a picture or diagram is worth a lot of explanation. Submit a photograph of a person with a learning disability using the WYNN terminal or a person who is blind using a refreshable Braille display.

Rebecca Davis, a program officer for the Public Welfare Foundation (PWF), proffered a list of items not to do when applying for an assistive-technology grant:[2]

1. Do not call anything unique; foundations prefer to fund things that are "part of the bigger picture."
2. Do not call yourselves the "only" anything.
3. Do not use the words *grow* or *impact* as verbs.
4. Do not use professional jargon.
5. Do not use fancy folders—a simple folder is preferred.

Step 2: Present Your Plan

Every funding agency has a mission statement and criteria for funding—pay close attention to these two items. By carefully reading these statements, you will able to identify keywords that when used will help you submit a funding request which has a better-than-average chance of being granted.

For example, when applying for a Technical Assistance Grant, which was established "to heighten the level of professional proficiency for library staff at an established library," it would behoove you to state, "We wish to increase services to the 10,000 patrons with disabilities who are part of our community. We would use our grant money to train a staff member to become proficient in using adaptive technology. This staff member would then write training manuals and instructions and train staff and patrons with disabilities (currently an underserved population) to use computers and the Internet. The end result would be patrons with disabilities being able to access the Web and enjoying the same opportunities as people without disabilities."

When applying for private grants, three letters of support or nominations are usually required. Ask a representative of the group you wish to serve to write one of the letters. In this letter, the representative can relate the "disenfranchisement" that he or she currently feels at not being able to freely access information and can say that adapted technology would remove many of the barriers to equal access to information.

Another letter of support should be written by a community volunteer organization, such as the Retired Seniors Volunteer Program (RSVP), which would state that it will provide support for the project by donating service hours to the library to assist paid staff. This is a big plus for grantors that want examples of "community cooperation" or "mentorship."

Do not, however, forget to include a letter of support from a professional in the library field. The funding organization will want to know that your peers agree that this is a good project and should receive a grant.

Step 3: Find the Right Funder

In these days of tight finances, this step becomes increasingly difficult, for many organizations are competing for the same funds. Rehabilitation centers and consumer groups are vying for the same dollars for identical purposes. There are still good starting sources for libraries, including those from the federal government.

Library Services and Technology Act (LSTA) Grants

Library Services and Technology Act (LSTA) grants are the major source of federal financing available for libraries. They are administered by the Institute of Museum and Library Services (IMLS) and replace the Library Services and Construction Act (LSCA) and Title II of the Higher Education Act (HEA). The LSTA grants require that the local funds must equal one-third of the amount of federal funds requested and may be in-kind or cash contributions. LSTA grants are competitive grants.

LSTA grants are essentially state-based programs that focus on "information access through technology" and "information empowerment through 'special services'." The emphasis is on public libraries, but it encourages partnerships among all libraries. Public, elementary, and school libraries; academic libraries; special libraries; and library consortiums are eligible to apply. Monies can be used to cover salaries, telecommunications equipment, and services.

Specific dates are set for submitting applications and for reports on the project's progress. For further information on your state's eligibility requirements or to apply for a grant, contact your state library or office of archives or the bureau that is designated to administer and grant federal funds. The Florida Department of State, Division of Library and Information Services, maintains an excellent information Website that includes guidelines and answers to frequently asked questions.[3]

Basic Library Service Grants

Basic Library Service Grants are small grant awards that support core library services on a noncompetitive basis. These grants are made to ensure that a minimum level of public library services is maintained for all citizens. Funds may be used to cover costs of salaries for library personnel, planning and needs assessments, in-service training of library personnel, library materials (including books, journals, electronic resources, and equipment), library supplies, and telecommunications services and equipment. For further information about applying for a grant, contact your state library or office of archives or the bureau that is designated to administer and grant federal funds.

Technical Assistance Grants

Technical Assistance Grants are awarded to raise the level of professional proficiency of library staff. These are small noncompetitive grants that will be used to provide support for a professional assessment of the effectiveness of "library operations that may include staffing, financial management, types and levels of services and collections, and management." An assessment of specialized operations may include "targeting library and information services to persons having difficulty using a library." For further information about applying for a Technical Assistance Grant, contact your state library or office of archives or the bureau that is designated to administer and grant federal funds.

Civic Clubs and Service Organization Grants

Civic organizations and foundations are excellent sources of funding projects such as library accessibility for persons with disabilities. While the grants may be small when compared with the total monies needed to make your library accessible, they should not be ignored. Oftentimes, social-service organizations (see figure 9-1) such as the Kiwanis and Lions will offer funding, providing matching funds are obtained.

These are only several organizations known to contribute; do not overlook fraternities or sororities that have community-service obligations. Or consider asking a local Boy Scout or Girl Scout troop to raise enough money to purchase Braille and large-print keytops, a worthy and obtainable goal for young people.

Information and Referral Programs

Several programs that do not offer funding may be able to refer you to state and local resources that do. These programs are the Alliance for Technology Access Resource Centers and the Technology Assistance Program (TAP). These programs do not exist in all states, but in those where they do, they may offer advice on locating funding for assistive technology and defining needs. They may be able to offer statistics to substantiate need.[4]

Disability Funding News

Also consider consulting *Disability Funding News,* a semimonthly report on "News, Views, Federal and Private Grants." This publication of CD Publications serves as a watchdog that monitors all resources relating to obtaining funding for persons with disabilities. It also alerts the readers to Senate and congressional bills that may affect services.

```
Muscular Dystrophy Association Affiliates
Catholic Charities
Chambers of Commerce
American Federation of Teachers
Elks Club
Lions Club
Labor Unions
American Red Cross
AARP
Kiwanis Clubs
Knights of Columbus
```

FIGURE 9-1
National and local organizations historically known to fund adaptive technology

The February 26, 1998, issue, for example, announced the availability of grants from the Department of Education for "Educational Department Competition for Rehabilitation Continuing Education"; private grants from "Kaman Corporation, Vulcan Materials Company, Medtronic Foundation, Baker Trust, Steelcase, TJX, SAFECO, NEC, and the Morgan Stanley Foundation."

On a regular basis the publication also offers "Grant Updates," "Grant Tips," and "Model Programs." Although the price tag of the publication may seem high, it does offer one-stop information on funding for adaptive technology.[5]

Keep Trying

If your grant application is not successful, do not hesitate to apply again. Ask for a list of candidates that were successful and, if possible, the application packages that they submitted to receive the grant. Compare these packages with the one you submitted. If you cannot discern the reason why theirs were successful and yours was not, approach the grant administrator and in a nonaccusatory manner ask him or her to explain the difference so that you may know how to proceed in submitting a successful application.

Notes

1. Many guides offer step-by-step suggestions for proposals, as does the World Wide Web. Certain sites offer online resources and technical help and often provide links and suggestions for potential funders. Key search words include "proposal writing," "grant making," and "adaptive technology."
2. "Welfare Foundation Offers Sound Advice on Increasing Odds for Winning Grants," *Disability Funding News,* February 26, 1998.

3. The Florida Government Information Locator Service can be found at <www.dos.state.fl.us/dlis/bid/grants>.
4. To locate the Alliance for Technology Access Resource Center in your state, visit its Website at <www.ataccess.org/atacenters>. To locate a TAP center in your state, contact the Rehabilitation Engineering and Assistive Technology Society of North America (RESNA) at its Website <www.resna.org/tap>.
5. *Disability Funding News* is a semimonthly publication available from CD Publications, 8204 Fenton Street, Silver Spring, MD 20910. For pricing information, contact them directly at the preceding address or call (301) 588-6380.

10

Making It All Work—Staff Training

With the intention of making a library facility one in which all will be able to access information, you may purchase every piece of adaptive equipment that your budget will allow and find that it is still not accessible to people with disabilities. The reason could be the environment created by the staff's attitude. Their attitude must be one that supports the addition of the equipment (and the workload) in a positive and knowledgeable manner. If this environment is not a nurturing one, people will not make a trip to your facility part of their routine.

Unfortunately, because we exist in a culture where stereotyping of people with disabilities is just now subsiding, sensitivity training for staff who will work in the environment (including also those who may not be on the building's physical staff but may be staff at an off-site help line for the equipment) is as mandatory as the training using the adaptive technology. A person who is blind can "see" body language and people who are "deaf" can hear sighs; therefore, it is important to take a day to instruct and remind staff about what constitutes quality service. In this discussion, various aspects of the term *service* must be included.

See the Person before the Disability

The entire staff must realize that people with disabilities are individuals who share many of the same goals, dreams, and desires as the staff members do. The only difference is the road of the disabled to the final destination may be slightly rougher. Everyone should also realize that people with disabilities share humanity's gifts of laughter and tears, pleasure and sorrow, and that they have the right to experience the full breadth of these emotions. People with disabilities can be male or female and can come in all shapes, sizes, races, and ages. The staff must appreciate that in the "blink of an eye," they, or someone they know, may become disabled and require specialized access considerations.

Basic Etiquette Must Be Followed

Even though each person and each disability will be dealt with on a one-to-one basis, there are general guidelines to follow. These guidelines were gleaned from publications produced by library systems and organizations for staff usage.[1]

BASIC CONSIDERATIONS WHEN ASSISTING PERSONS WITH DISABILITIES

1. Be natural when working with a person with a disability; do not overcompensate. It's OK to say "See you later" to a person who is blind.
2. Talk directly to the person with the disability unless it is impossible.
3. Offer your assistance rather than assisting.
4. When unsure of how to proceed in a situation, ask the person for advice.
5. Do not estrange persons with disabilities from persons without disabilities. For instance, if a blind person is waiting in line to check out an audio-described video, do not bring him or her to the front of the line; it would be helpful, however, to tell that person that there probably will be a five-minute wait.
6. Remember, there are invisible disabilities, such as hearing impairments, that might cause you to be asked to repeat a question in a different manner.
7. Be patient. It may take longer for persons with disabilities to complete a necessary task, such as signing their names. If they are attempting to do what is asked, let them. Do not say, "that's all right," just to speed up the process.
8. Refer to the person's disability only if it is relevant to the conversation.
9. Use correct language concerning disabilities whenever possible.
10. Treat adults with disabilities as adults and children with disabilities as children.

Special Considerations When Assisting Patrons Who Are Blind or Visually Impaired

The approach to rendering services to persons who are blind or visually impaired will vary with the individual. Certain individuals who are very independent will desire a minimal amount of individual training. Conversely, some individuals will require step-by-step tutorials. Solutions for individual scenarios cannot be offered; however, there are basic rules to remember when assisting persons who are blind or visually impaired.

THINGS TO REMEMBER WHEN ASSISTING PEOPLE WITH VISUAL IMPAIRMENTS

1. When approaching persons who are visually impaired or blind, greet them and identify yourself. You may then inquire about the type of help needed.
2. Offer the person your arm and proceed to walk a half step ahead. Warn the person when floor levels change. If offering a chair, indicate exactly where the chair is in relation to where the person is standing.
3. When orientating the person to the library environment, use specific directions. If the person is to follow a path and make a turn, say walk "ten steps and make a right turn."
4. When orientating persons on the computer, it is also necessary to be specific. Rather than simply saying, "press <ALT>, <SHIFT>, <DEL>," you should add "which on this keyboard are next to the space bar, two keys over and one up. . . ."
5. When you are leaving the area, let the person know so he or she will not continue a conversation.
6. Never pet or disturb a guide dog.

Service Considerations When Assisting Persons Who Have Hearing Impairments

Deafness and other severe hearing impairments are considered two of the "invisible disabilities." (Others include learning disability, epilepsy, diabetes, etc.) Many times people who are deaf will visit the library without anyone being aware of their visit. Deafness is invisible when you are talking to someone who you feel simply "isn't listening to you." In reality, such a person may not be "hearing" you.

The degree of hearing impairment and the individual will determine what special services will be needed.

Following are some basic things to remember when interacting with persons who are hearing impaired.

THINGS TO REMEMBER WHEN ASSISTING PEOPLE WITH HEARING IMPAIRMENTS

1. Deaf people use a variety of ways to communicate, such as lipreading, sign language, speaking, and writing. All techniques are visual, however, so be careful not to turn your face away while speaking.
2. Be sure you have the person's attention. You can wave your hand, touch a person's shoulder, or tap on the table.
3. Always speak directly to the disabled person, not to the person accompanying him or her.
4. Maintain eye contact; do not cover your lips in any manner. If you have a lozenge in your mouth, remove it when speaking to afford a full view of your facial movements.
5. If you have trouble being understood, rephrase your statement using different words. For example, if when telling a person the fee is "50 cents," he or she hears "15 cents," repeat the amount using "half a dollar." It is acceptable to write a note.
6. Speak clearly and not too fast. Consonants, especially, should be articulated; however, care should be taken not to overarticulate.
7. If a long conversation is foreseen (i.e., instructions), move to a word processor and type your communication.

Special Considerations When Assisting Persons with Mobility Impairments

Mobility impairments is a term used to describe any disability that prohibits the use of a person's own limbs to move about. The person may need to use a wheelchair or may be able to use a cane or walker to move about. Each individual person will need a specific solution. Following are some tips to remember when working with persons with mobility impairments.

THINGS TO REMEMBER WHEN ASSISTING PEOPLE WITH MOBILITY IMPAIRMENTS

1. If the person with a mobility impairment is using a wheelchair, do not assume you may purposefully touch the chair. The wheelchair, in a manner of speaking, is acting as a person's "legs" and is part of his or her personal space.

2. Speak directly to the person in the wheelchair. If a long conversation is foreseen, try to sit to prevent the wheelchair user from being forced to constantly look up to maintain eye contact.
3. Know which tables a person in a wheelchair can slide under. Also be aware of which chairs are stable enough and provide support for patrons using wheelchairs to safely transfer themselves.
4. Be sure the directions you give are accessible.

Special Considerations When Assisting Persons with Learning Disabilities

Individuals with learning disabilities usually will not appear to be any different than persons without disabilities. They simply process materials and information differently. The type of learning disability each individual possesses will dictate the type of assistance he or she needs. Remembering basics will make everyone feel comfortable.

THINGS TO REMEMBER WHEN ASSISTING PEOPLE WITH LEARNING DISABILITIES

1. Some patrons with learning disabilities may not be able to read printed instructions and will need to have them read aloud.
2. It may be necessary to explain what you are saying using different words. In some cases it may be necessary to present a written explanation as well as an oral explanation.
3. Some types of learning disabilities cause individuals to become easily distracted. You may need to signal the patron via a light tap on the computer screen to focus his or her attention to the text on the computer screen.
4. Try to eliminate all outside distractions by conducting the instructions in an area that is less traveled. Less traveled, however, does not mean isolated.

Introducing Staff to Persons with Disabilities

In the course of staff training, a key element is introducing staff to people who are disabled. Many people with visual impairments are just beginning to return to public libraries. Some staff may simply feel uncomfortable and afraid of interactions because they feel they may say the wrong thing.

While presenting a "dog and pony show" is not advised, consider asking your advisory committee (as well as any guests they might think appropriate) to make a friendly presentation to the staff. They should, in their own words, be able to tell staff what their needs are and how they expect them to be addressed. Staff, in turn, will be welcomed to respond. Stereotypes and assumptions will soon disappear as the dialogue continues. If time and funds permit, a "shared" coffee or luncheon break should be included so staff and patrons can talk on an informal basis. Very often, the simple process of sharing food and drink makes everyone realize that we are basically the same.

Knowing What Adaptive Devices Are Available

Because budget cuts and downsizing are the norm, it is unlikely that additional staff will be hired to specifically work with the adaptive technology. Thus, it is necessary for staff to make the concept manageable as part of a workday. The staff needs to know what equipment is available, how to use the equipment, and how to instruct patrons on using the equipment.

Professional Training

Obtain professional training for all the adaptive equipment you purchase. If you buy a large amount of equipment, vendors will be happy to include a training seminar with the equipment purchase. While it may not be possible to involve all staff in the original vendor training, include as many of the public-service staff as possible. Consider asking the vendor to allow videotaping and audiotaping of the demonstration for later use. Most vendors will be happy to comply with this request and may be willing to help you index the presentation with the hope of saving service calls to their help lines.

Include members of your advisory board and potential volunteers in these training sessions. Members of this consumer group may pick up different aspects and approaches to use than a staff focused on the demonstration as an added task.

Allow each employee to have hands-on experience with the equipment. If at all possible, schedule all public staff to actually sit down and use the equipment on a fairly regular basis until using the equipment becomes nonintimidating.

Other Learning Aids for Staff and Patrons

Many manufacturers provide tutorials with their products that act as mentors when personal teachers are not available. Also, many times people feel more comfortable receiving instructions from a volunteer rather than from paid staff, for they feel they may be taking too much time in learning a task. The tutorials and instructions should be kept in an accessible area within the workstation.

Disabilities, Opportunities, Internetworking, and Technology (DO-IT)

"Universal Access: Electronic Resources in Libraries" is an excellent training module on the concept of access to libraries for persons with disabilities. It was developed by Disabilities, Opportunities, Internetworking, and Technology (DO-IT) in cooperation with Computing and Communications and University Libraries at the University of Washington. Its aim is to help librarians familiarize their staffs with electronic resources that help make libraries accessible to persons with disabilities. The project was funded by the Dole Foundation's Telecommunications Funding Project and the NSF.

The training presentation offers the user advice on conducting various in-service training sessions. Leaders have the option of simply showing a 20-minute video and distributing brochures as a quick overview or conducting a one-and-a-half to two-hour presentation to describe concepts of adaptive technology and accessible Web design. The options of conducting half- or full-day workshops that fully explore the integration of adaptive technology and universal design are also included.

DO-IT's instructions are very specific. DO-IT assumes that the presentor probably does not have time to prepare a formal presentation, so it includes materials that can be used to make overhead transparencies. A script for the presentation and discussion topics on various disabilities are included in the presentation package.

This unique tool is available in print from DO-IT and the ALA. An electronic version of the project is also available at DO-IT's Website.[2]

Accessible Step-by-Step Instructions for Speech Technology (ASSIST)—Iowa Department for the Blind Tutorials

The Iowa Department for the Blind received a Special Project Grant from the U.S. Department of Education to develop a series of tutorials that acquaint the novice speech-access user to a variety of screen readers in Windows environments. ASSIST is an acronym (the Iowa Department for the Blind thinks this may be the longest acronym) that stands for Accessible Step-by-Step Instructions for Speech Technology.

ASSIST has developed tutorials for the following screen readers: JAWS, Windows Bridge, and WinVision. They are available free of charge (on diskette or cassette or downloadable) from the Iowa Department for the Blind.[3]

The Iowa Department for the Blind Website is also a model for those wishing to create an accessible Website. In addition to offering a site map, this Iowa Website states and describes its accessibility features, which makes it a good site to emulate.

WebABLE Classes

The Yuri Rubinsky Insight Foundation hosts the WebABLE site, which offers seminars and conferences at various venues throughout the world.[4] It offers on-site training. The Website, in addition to offering hyperlink access to hundreds of disability orientated sites, offers a summation of various presentations made during the past two years. Although an on-site tutorial session may be cost-prohibitive for one organization, consider asking several other smaller organizations (using the same equipment) to cosponsor training.

NFB Net

Hosted by the National Federation of the Blind (NFB), NFB Net allows anyone to Telnet-access the tutorials via a shell or PPP connection.[5] Subjects covered are the use of adaptions to access Windows-based programs.

Rewriting Instructions

Instructions written by software and hardware developers are rarely usable by novice users. The people who have been taught (or who have taught themselves) should compile a set of simple instructions that will allow the new user to use the adaptive equipment on his or her first attempt. Nothing can dissuade use more than handing a patron a 12-page manual and saying, "Everything you need is right in here." Better to hand him or her one sheet of instructions (or a recorded cassette of instructions) and say, "These instructions will get you started and allow you to practice. . . . When you feel like moving into the more intricate procedures, the manual will be on your right."

A good test is to ask a patron (not necessarily a potential user) to follow the instructions exactly. Request that the user write down any step he or she may have had to fill in for himself or herself, even obvious commands such as Turn on PC or Hit the Return. Remember that all users may not visually see that the computer is not turned on or may have conceptual disabilities that do not tell them that they must press <RETURN> when they are finished with the input.

Attending Workshops and Seminars

Locating a workshop or seminar on adaptive accessibility to the Internet and computers will mean leaving the mainstream. While the ALA frequently presents annual programs on service to persons with disabilities and adaptive technology, the programs are not able to cover the entire spectrum.

Closing the Gap

The annual Closing the Gap conference is sponsored by the journal *Closing the Gap: Computer Technology for People with Special Needs,* headquartered in Minneapolis, Minnesota. The conference has an international reputation as a leading source for information on innovative applications of computer technology for persons with disabilities. Workshops with hands-on opportunities are offered.

Topics discussed cover the gamut of the "technology for the disabled" issues, but enough programs on the topic of "adapted access to information" make attendance worthwhile. Because the presentations are made by people with disabilities, special educators, personnel managers, government officials, and hardware/software developers, there are tremendous opportunities for networking and gathering information. Closing the Gap's annual conference also allows attendees to view a large display of adapted devices in the exhibits area.

The conference is held in Minnesota in October. Contact Closing the Gap for exact dates.[6]

California State University Northridge (CSUN)

The Center on Disabilities, California State University Northridge (CSUN), has hosted the CSUN annual conference on Technology and Persons with Disabilities for 13 years. The conference, usually held in the fall, provides a forum for educators, project site developers, consumers, Web developers, Internet-access specialists, and hardware and software developers to explain what they did to make their sites, information, and products more accessible. Most presentations will also include problems encountered and resolutions. CSUN does have a Website with abstracts of presentations for the past two years.[7]

Equal Access to Software and Information (EASI)

Equal Access to Software and Information (EASI) has several online workshops that focus on adaptive computing technology, creating accessible Web pages and learning disabilities. Workshop "attendees" use the Internet and e-mail to participate in courses such as "ADAPT-IT," which is a four-week course that provides an overview on computing and focuses on setting up computing technology and services for individuals with disabilities.

Listing Available Equipment

All staff should know what type of equipment the library owns. The most thorough way to do this is to prepare an illustrated listing of each piece of equipment owned. In addition to a photograph of the device, include the type of equipment (for example, book reader), where it is located, its intended use, any available tutorials and other information that would be helpful for staff to know.

As you compile this information, keep in mind that this listing can serve as an important marketing tool. Prepare the document in a manner and format that is accessible by persons with various levels of intellectual comprehension. An excellent example of a document that works was prepared by the Lee County Florida Library System in 1996.[8] Entitled "Catalog of Assistive Devices for Seniors and Persons with Disabilities," the document is produced in large print and clearly shows a picture of the assistive device, a thorough description of what the device does, its size, and the potential user.

If you have a Website, add the listing of adaptive equipment in a format that is usable by the equipment you are discussing.

As the staff becomes more familiar and at ease with the new equipment, they may actively seek out ways to improve and expand services. Certainly, all staff will receive personal satisfaction when they assist a patron in formatting and printing his or her first Braille document.

Notes

1. Mid-Hudson Library System, "Now That We've Met, What Do I Say? General Guidelines for Communication with Persons Who Have Disabilities," Mid-Hudson Library System, Outreach Services Department, Poughkeepsie, New York, 1994; University of Toronto, "Making Connections: A Guide for Library Staff Serving Persons with Disabilities," Toronto, Ontario, Canada, 1994; DO-IT, University of Washington, "Making Library Resources Accessible to People with Disabilities," Seattle, Washington, 1997; Ohio Library Council, "Assisting the Patron with . . ." series; Columbus, Ohio, Outreach and Special Services Section, 1993.
2. DO-IT's electronic presentation of Universal Access: Electronic Resources in Libraries is available at <www.weber.u.washington.edu/~doit/UA/>.

3. For a free copy of the tutorials, contact the Iowa Department of the Blind at: ASSIST with Windows, Iowa Department for the Blind, 524 Fourth Street, Des Moines, IA 50309-2364; or call (512) 281-1333; or visit their Website at <www.blind.state.ia.us/assist>.
4. The Yuri Rabinsky Insight Foundation is located at <www.Yuri.org/webable>.
5. David Andrews, "NFB NET Training Seminar," *Braille Monitor* (April 1998): 167–68. To learn more about the tutorials, visit the NFB Website at <www.NBF.org>.
6. For more information on Closing the Gap, contact Closing the Gap, 526 Main Street, P.O. Box 68, Henderson, MN 56044; or call (507) 248-3294; or visit their Website at <www.closingthegap.com>.
7. For more information on the CSUN conference, contact CSUN Conference, California State University, Northridge, 18111 Nordhoff Street, Northridge, CA 91330-8340; or call (818) 677-2578; or visit their Website at <www.dinf.org/csun>.
8. The Lee County Florida Library System created the catalog as part of "Library Access for All, Year 2," a project that provides improved access to library services for persons with disabilities. The project was partially funded by a federal LSCA grant. Lee County received an Association of Specialized and Cooperative Library Agencies (ASCLA)/J.C. Penney National Organization for Disability Award for this project in 1997. For further information on the catalog, write the Lee County Florida Library System in care of The Talking Books Library, 13249 North Cleveland Avenue, #5–6, North Fort Meyers, FL 33903.

11

Announcing Improved Access

Often, facilities that purchase adaptive equipment lament that the devices are being underutilized or not used at all. Frequently, the reason for the equipment not being used is that no one knows it is there. Several generations of people with disabilities do not think that public or academic libraries provide materials that they can independently access. Many of these people will not not magically appear in a library unless the word is out that something is new in the library, something exciting and enlightening. Develop a marketing plan that will sell the library, staff, and the materials within to a population waiting to be served.

Hosting a Family Kickoff Program and Open House

Everyone appreciates a celebration and what better way to celebrate than to have a family-day celebration to show off and tell all about the library's equipment? By using the "family-sharing" theme, both elders with visual impairments and children with learning disabilities can explore adapted computer access together, each helping the other.

Getting the word out to the right people requires planning and hard work. While a significant number of libraries have an active marketing plan, most libraries do not. The theory is that librarians and information providers feel that their product is so valuable (and it is) that it should simply sell itself. Unfortunately, all persons do not understand the possibilities and promises of libraries. Therefore, it is necessary to develop an active "notification plan" to alert this group that technologies are available that will help them access print information.

Mass Media—Local Newspapers, Radio, and Television

The media is a strong vehicle for letting the populace know that something is new at the library. Virtually everyone knows someone who is learning disabled or visually impaired and can benefit from the newly installed technologies, and would be glad to pass the message on to the appropriate party. In the larger markets, however, competition is fierce for air or print space and it is hard for libraries to convince unenlightened program directors or editors that "library news" is important. In these cases, libraries must submit to employing attention-getting tactics.

Consider sending a press release in a form other than standard print. A Braille letter will still get the attention of inquiring minds. Equally attention-getting would be a taped version of the press release using a speech synthesizer. And tired eyes would surely appreciate the press release in large print as well as in standard print. The four formats of the press release as a packet are bound to make an impact on at least one of the media who receive the press release.

More Specialized Media—Radio Reading Services

Radio Reading Services is a network of low-frequency broadcasting stations dedicated to "providing" newspapers to clients who have a receiver set to the proper frequency. Radio Reading Services has transmitters in most urban areas and in many rural communities. Many Radio Reading Services will be glad to read your news release as a public service. If you are unable to locate a Radio Reading Service near you, contact your local Sight Rehabilitation Center or Regional Library for the Blind and Physically Handicapped for a contact.

Senior Clubs, Senior Housing Units, and the Parent and Teacher Associations

While it may not seem that senior clubs and parenting associations have anything in common, they both are good venues for the word-of-mouth advertising that remains a very reliable marketing tool. Ask to speak at senior citizens and school meetings to announce the new items you have acquired to aid in accessing information. Seniors whose eyesight has diminished will be relieved that the CCTV you purchased will allow them to read their correspondence themselves and retain their independence. Parents of children with learning disabilities will be elated when they hear that you have acquired the hardware and software that allow their children to access the Internet. Neither of these groups will need any encouragement to "spread the news."

When making your presentation, bring detailed, illustrated brochures that highlight and explain the new technologies for distribution. If there isn't room on the meeting agenda for you to speak, ask that you be allowed to post an informational flier on a bulletin board or write a notice in the organization's newsletter.

Churches, Temples, and Other Places of Worship

Places of worship, as a whole, are inclusionary and have tried to make their facilities as accessible as possible. Many have purchased large-print hymnals and prayer books. Additionally, many organizations produce and distribute materials in special media. It is only natural that they would be helpful in getting out the word about the adaptions at the library that allow their members to access text.

Ask the organization's spiritual leader to post your information in the church bulletin, which in some cases is produced in special media. A creative leader may be able to work the announcement into a "lesson."

Consumer Groups

American Council of the Blind (ACB)

The American Council of the Blind (ACB) is a nonprofit organization comprised of "tens of thousands" of blind, visually impaired, and sighted individuals throughout the United States. The ACB has 51 state and regional affiliates that focus on improving the quality of life at the local level. They maintain a strong lobby effort on both the national and local levels to ensure that the rights of individuals who are visually impaired or blind are not usurped.

Most of the local ACB chapters meet monthly and the state chapters produce newsletters in special formats and would be happy to inform their members about your facility's innovations. Additionally, the ACB holds an annual conference that includes several sessions on adaptive technology and computer access to the Internet. If you cannot locate a chapter near your site, the national headquarters would be happy to assist you.[1]

National Federation of the Blind (NFB)

The NFB is a nonprofit organization comprised of 50,000 members in all 50 states, plus Washington, D.C., and Puerto Rico. Seven hundred local chapters function as consumer and advocacy organizations. The purpose of the NFB "is twofold—to help blind persons achieve self-confidence and self-respect and to act as a vehicle for collective self-expression by the blind."

They seek to accomplish their goals through public education about blindness, information and referral services, scholarships, aids and appliances, and the evaluation of technology. The local chapters hold monthly meetings and the state chapters meet annually. The state chapters publish monthly newsletters and would be eager to inform members about your facility's technology developments. The NFB's annual conference includes presentations on technology and Internet access. If you cannot locate a chapter near your site, contact the national headquarters and they will be glad to assist you in finding one.[2]

Veterans of Foreign Wars (VFW)

Veterans groups should also receive notifications of your enhancements. Many of our veterans received their respective disabilities from participating in military service. Fliers posted on bulletin boards will be read. Many able-bodied vets will be glad to share news of service enhancements at your facility. Contact your local Veterans of Foreign Wars (VFW) chapter to see if you can speak at a local meeting.

Learning Disability Association Contacts

Because the term *learning disabilities* is used as a generic term, the contacts are diverse. You will, however, find a group of educators, parents, and persons with learning differences within the membership.

The Orton Dyslexia Society of the Learning Disabilities Association of America (LDAA) has chapters throughout the United States. Topics of discussion often include information, resources for parents and professionals, research, technology, and legislation. Monthly meetings are held at the state level and speakers are welcome. You will find this group extremely receptive to learning that adaptive equipment has been installed in their neighborhood. If you cannot locate a chapter near your site, contact the national headquarters of the Orton Dyslexia Society of the LDAA.[3]

Additionally, ALA's project, "Roads to Learning," hosts a Website, "Internet Resources for Learning Disabilities and Related Topics," that has many links to resources concerning learning disabilities. The few minutes spent searching this Website will provide you with other groups in your area concerned with access for persons with learning disabilities.[4]

The mission of Self-Help for Hard-of-Hearing People (SHHH) is to make a difference in the areas of access, awareness, and educational concerns for people who are hard of hearing. More than 250 SHHH affiliates are located in 49 states, with more chapters planned. The chapters publish newsletters that are very amenable to posting information relating to added access. You may also wish to address a chapter meeting to explain how some of the adapted devices you purchased work. If you cannot locate a chapter near your site, contact the national headquarters and they will be glad to assist you in finding one.[5]

Rehabilitation Centers

Most metropolitan areas have a vision or general rehabilitation center located within their environs. Many mobile individuals frequent these centers for both educational and social interactions. All would welcome a book and informational talk during one of their meetings.

Vision and rehabilitation centers that are sufficiently funded will also produce and mail out informational fliers to their registered clients and will be happy to include information about your facility in their newsletters. Also contact the mobility instructor at the vision center in case directions to your facility may be needed by clients in the near future. Consult your local phone book for addresses.

Independent Living Centers (ILC)

Independent Living Centers (ILC) are a means for persons with disabilities to "control and direct their own lives." People who receive services from the centers generally are active and strive for mobility and learning, and simply need referrals to resources that offer daily living assistance. Many of the centers do publish newsletters and are glad to pass on positive news that will interest their clients. If you cannot locate centers near you, ADA Access maintains a state directory on its Website.[6]

Network Libraries for the Blind and Physically Handicapped

Often forgotten as a marketing device are state and network library newsletters. While these newsletters are not patron-oriented, they help spread the news via word of mouth from librarians in a neighboring county system to a colleague in your county (but not necessarily your system), who is glad to refer a patron who needs to use adapted technology not owned by his or her library to your site.

Almost all network libraries serving the blind and physically handicapped have newsletters that are produced in special media. They would be pleased to print your announcement in their newsletters. Many, as their time permits, may even be willing to mail your announcements to their registered patrons in your area. If you do not know the location of the library in your service area, contact the NLS for the Blind and Physically Handicapped.[7]

Local Advertising Circulars and Supermarkets

Two very inexpensive ways to let your residents know what is available in your library are linked to two very real life experiences—saving money and shopping for food. Every week brings some type of "local merchant coupon and advertising booklet" to the mailbox. Advertising in these booklets is very inexpensive, and they are accessed by recipients eager to save money on a meal or an oil change. Family and friends of individuals with disabilities are sure to notice a message that states, "Having trouble reading small print? Morepower Public Library has new machines that may be able to help you access print."

Notices posted on bulletin boards or coupon-exchange counters of the local supermarkets will also be seen by many. If your budget allows, inexpensive magnifiers with your library's name, address, phone number, and the message of "larger magnifying devices available at our facility" will also send a message that will be "picked up and stored for future reference."

Community Websites

What better place to share information about new technology but through technology? People who surf the Web are generally information seekers and sharers who are glad to pass on any information about technology to others. Although they may not need adaptive technology themselves, they may be enticed into the library to try the new equipment and may like it enough to stay and become a volunteer trainer.

Posting additional services of local Websites and free-nets is also a good way to show taxpayers that you are being responsive to all community members.

After you have mailed out all your invitations and hosted the kickoff party, keep in contact with your potential audience. Fliers in special media announcing new products or Websites of interest are a good method of completing this task. Continue to observe rules of courtesy and ask patrons to pass the "accessibility word" on to others.

Notes

1. Contact the national headquarters of the ACB at ACB, 1155 15th Street, N.W., Suite 720, Washington, DC 20005; or call (800) 424-8666 or (202) 467-5081; or visit their Website at <www.ACB.org>.
2. Contact the National Federation for the Blind at NFB, 1800 Johnson Street, Baltimore, MD 21230; or call (410) 659-9314; or visit their Website at <www.nfb.org>.
3. Contact the LDA at LDA, 4156 Library Road, Pittsburgh, PA 15234-1349; or visit its Website at <www.ldanatl.org/lda>.
4. Visit the ALA Roads to Learning "Internet Resources for Learning Disabilities and Related Topics" at <www.ala.org/roads>.
5. Contact SHHH at Self-Help for Hard-of-Hearing People, Inc., 7910 Woodmont Avenue, Suite 1200, Bethesda, MD 20814; or call (301) 657-2248; by TTY at (301) 657-2249; or visit their Website at <www.shhh.org>.
6. The ADA Access Website can be found at <www.adaaccess.com>.
7. Contact the NLS at National Library Service for the Blind and Physically Handicapped at (202) 707-5100 or visit their Website at <lcweb.loc.gov/nls>, which has all address and phone numbers of the network libraries and hyperlinks to those with Websites.

12 Working in the Real World

In an ideal world, library managers would not have problems with getting the dollars needed to build and staff libraries adequately and appropriately. They would not have to be concerned about equipment budgets, payroll costs, and building limitations. In an ideal world, library managers would be able to set up workstations that would accommodate all users with a wide array of disabilities. In an ideal world, we would simply order one of everything and hire an automation specialist to maintain the equipment and a staff to train patrons in using the equipment. In an ideal world, no one would be denied independent access to computers and information.

Library managers, however, do not live in an ideal world, but rather they live in the real world. Library systems must constantly battle for budget allocations from governmental agencies and work to get tax levies and grant applications approved. Only with rare exceptions will libraries be able to do all that they want to do when they want to do it. So they, much like corporations and businesses, need to develop long- and short-range goals. This is a good method for phasing in adaptive technology.

Start with a Plan

Kelly Pierce, Disability Specialist at the Cook County State's Attorney's Office, Chicago, Illinois, offers suggestions for developing a workable plan.[1]

BASIC CONSIDERATIONS FOR GOAL PLANNING

1. Form an advisory committee consisting of potential users. Be deliberate in choosing the makeup by selecting people from various age

groups (include parents of children with disabilities) and disabilities. Be careful, however, not to make the committee too large and be sure to include your automation staff, business manager, and marketing specialist.

2. Assess the capabilities and willingness of your automation staff. Are they willing to learn the mechanics of adaptive technology even though the staff's workload already is heavy? Are they comfortable taking suggestions from adaptive-technology specialists who may not be on staff and have disabilities?
3. Find an adaptive-technology vendor with whom you have a comfortable working relationship and one who offers training and a commitment to helping you find broad-based solutions. Very often, adaptive-technology vendors are technology users themselves. Be sure to take advantage of this situation to avoid possible pitfalls.
4. Determine what skills you and your staff need to learn to operate each piece of equipment you intend to purchase.
5. Focus on function—determine which adaptive devices can be used by the greatest cross section of consumers with disabilities.
6. Focus on function—determine which adaptive devices can be used by persons without disabilities when not being used by persons with disabilities.
7. Read independent evaluations of the equipment you intend to purchase. Be sure that the persons writing the reviews are either users or instructors. Do not be swayed by job titles. If possible, find out the age, educational background, and experience of each person evaluating the product. Creating a miniportrait of the reviewer gives you a better focal point when reading the review.
8. Ask for on-site demonstrations and trial usage of some of the equipment you wish to purchase. This will allow your advisory committee to test the items and comment.
9. Strive for simplicity. Keeping solutions simple reduces maintenance and repair.
10. Think and plan; avoid stereotyped solutions. Remember that while disabilities are seemingly different, the solutions to allowing access may be the same.

Following these sensible steps will enable you to determine the right adaptive equipment for your patrons and your budget. These steps will enable you to develop reachable short-term goals while pursuing your long-range goals.

Ten Recommended Short-Term Goals

The goals that follow are suggestions of the author and DO-IT; you will need to adapt them to fit your situation.[2]

SUGGESTIONS FOR SHORT-TERM PLANS

1. One of the very first goals is making your Website accessible. Be sure that people using adaptive equipment to access the Internet are not faced with obstacles. This is not a costly measure and could be acted on immediately.
2. Train staff. Staff must embrace the idea of added accessibility, know how to use the equipment, and how best to interact with special populations.
3. Take an inventory of accessibility products on-site. Many sites are using products such as Internet Explorer and Netscape that already have accessibility attributes which could be activated. Explore the possibilities and write procedures that could be used to activate them. Develop a policy that allows people with disabilities to use the configurations (i.e., who can enter the keystrokes that activate the programs?). For instance, users who are deaf would be aided by Microsoft's SoundSentry alerting device, but would they know it's available and could be activated?
4. Find an accessible location for your adaptive workstations so that people using wheelchairs or walkers will be able to find them and sit at them.
5. Purchase large monitors of at least 19 inches and large-print keytop labels. These will allow patrons with low vision and learning disabilities to access the database with greater ease.
6. Buy a speech system and inexpensive software such as PwWebSpeak. This equipment will allow access to the Web by patrons with low vision, blindness, and learning disabilities.
7. Procure screen-enlarging software and adapt printers to produce large print. This will allow easier access to the Internet by persons with visual impairments and learning disabilities and allow them to read the output. Most laser jet printers can be programmed to produce large print.
8. Purchase Braille conversion software and a Braille output device. Braille users will gain independent use of all databases. If a Braille printer cannot be purchased, establish a policy that will allow a patron to copy findings onto a diskette. A diskette-exchange program is recommended to avoid viruses (the patron's disk can better be scanned for viruses during off-hours).
9. Buy an alternate input device. This could be a speech-recognition system, a trackball, or a membrane keyboard. This addition would help people with limited physical strength or learning disabilities to access the Internet.
10. Procure a reading system. As these systems become more efficient and less expensive, they can be added to your equipment inventory.

Long-Term Goal

One major long-term goal would simply be to build on the goals listed previously and acquire a sufficient number in direct proportion to your user population. If you are in an area with an older population, be sure that you have enough large monitors; if you are in an area with a youthful population, be sure that there are enough workstations with adaptions that aid persons with learning disabilities. Also plan on adding staff and volunteers to the team.

When making your library computer accessible to disabled patrons, in addition to determining short- and long-term goals, you should consider certain basics during your planning process.

GENERAL TIPS FOR PLANNING

1. Be sure to include reachable short-term goals to help maintain a positive attitude.
2. Be aware that you will need more than one adapted workstation to accommodate all needs. Remember, the more access tools installed on one system, the more compatability problems you will encounter. These problems include running out of memory or a patron wishing to use one program but accidently choosing another.
3. Develop an access menu for each adaptive program you purchase.
4. Develop a security plan that will allow users to make needed changes to displays, but that will protect the library. Consider issuing passwords to patrons who will need to customize their displays, using resident programs available in browsers such as Internet Explorer or Navigator.
5. Develop a plan for people to take copy with them in needed media. If a Braille printer is not available, allow users to copy material to diskettes. You should institute a diskette-exchange program. A diskette-exchange program allows you to avoid viruses by giving the patron a virusfree diskette and checking the patron's diskette when time allows.
6. Follow the leader. Find a library that has successfully accomplished some of your goals. Contact it and ask how it was done, as well as any other questions you may have. Remember, answering questions and giving directions are part of a library's mission.

Libraries Committed to Universal Access

The following libraries represent a cross section that is making efforts to ensure that all members of the community they serve are able to access information. These libraries were brought to the attention of the author in various ways, but mainly through word of mouth—people and patrons who justifiably have something good to say about these institutions. With one exception, these institutions did not have a "fairy godmother" wave a magic wand to make their buildings and computer systems accessible. They did it by planning, creative budgeting, and hard work.

Librarians were asked various questions, such as the equipment that is available, the policies for using the equipment, the costs of the equipment, the source of their funding, the staff training that is required, and the usage by the community. A staff name was also provided for those who may wish to contact someone for advice. This information is presented in detail in Appendix 3.

All of the libraries are not at the same level of access to information and are included to illustrate that any organization can start the process and attain ongoing success.

COLLEGE CENTER for LIBRARY AUTOMATION (CCLA)
1238 Blountstown Highway
Tallahassee, Florida 32304
Voice: (850) 922-6044
Website: <www.ccla.lib.fl.us>

SAN JOSE STATE UNIVERSITY LIBRARY (SJSUL)
One Washington Square
San Jose, California 95192-0028
Voice: (408) 924-2818
Library Website: <www.library.sjsu.edu>
Disability Resource Center (DRC) Website: <www.drc.sjsu.edu>
City of San Jose Website that cites disability access design standards: <www.ci.sanjose.ca.us/oaacc/disacces>

SAN FRANCISCO PUBLIC LIBRARY
Blind Services Center and Deaf Services Center
100 Larken Street
Civic Center
San Francisco, California 94102
Voice: (415) 557-4253; TTD: (415) 557-4433
Website: <www.sfpl.lib.ca.us>

SEATTLE PUBLIC LIBRARY
Library Equal Access Program (LEAP)
1000 4th Avenue
Seattle, Washington 98104
Voice: (206) 386-4690
Website: <www.spl.org>

JOHNSON COUNTY LIBRARY
9875 West 87th Street
Overland Park, Kansas 66212
Voice: (913) 495-2400
Website: <www.jcl.lib.ks.us>

FAIRFAX COUNTY LIBRARY
Access Services
12000 Government Center Parkway, Suite 123
Fairfax, Virginia 22035-0012
Voice: (703) 324-8380; TTY: (703) 324-8635
Website: <www.co.fairfax.va.us/library>

"Cyberlibraries" Offering Outstanding Accessible Websites

While many public and academic libraries are offering Websites and gateways, few are offering sites that are accessible to those using adaptive equipment. The reason for this is that librarians, wishing to show that libraries are "cool" and "happening," avail themselves of all the glamour and gizmos to entice the masses. The following library Websites are favorites with users of screen readers and adaptive technology.

Cleveland Public Library

<www.cpl.org>

The Cleveland Public Library has organized its Website to emulate the actual physical library that hosts the site. Once the user chooses the Electronic Resources option (see figure 12-1), he or she is presented with a listing of virtual departments. These departments are simply listed in one column, which correctly is aligned to the left screen margin.

Links to sites are cataloged within these subject departments. For instance, choosing the History and Geography department (see figure 12-2) will present the user with links to logical divisions within that department.

Because the subjects are aligned to the left, all the user needs to do is <PAGE DOWN> until the general subject he or she is looking for appears. In this case, the subject quest is Vietnam, so the user would choose Eurasia & Oceania. The user is then presented with the Eurasia & Oceania menu as in figure 12-3 (again, note a single column, aligned left, is presented).

This allows the user of adaptive technology to scroll down until the subject of Vietnam is found.

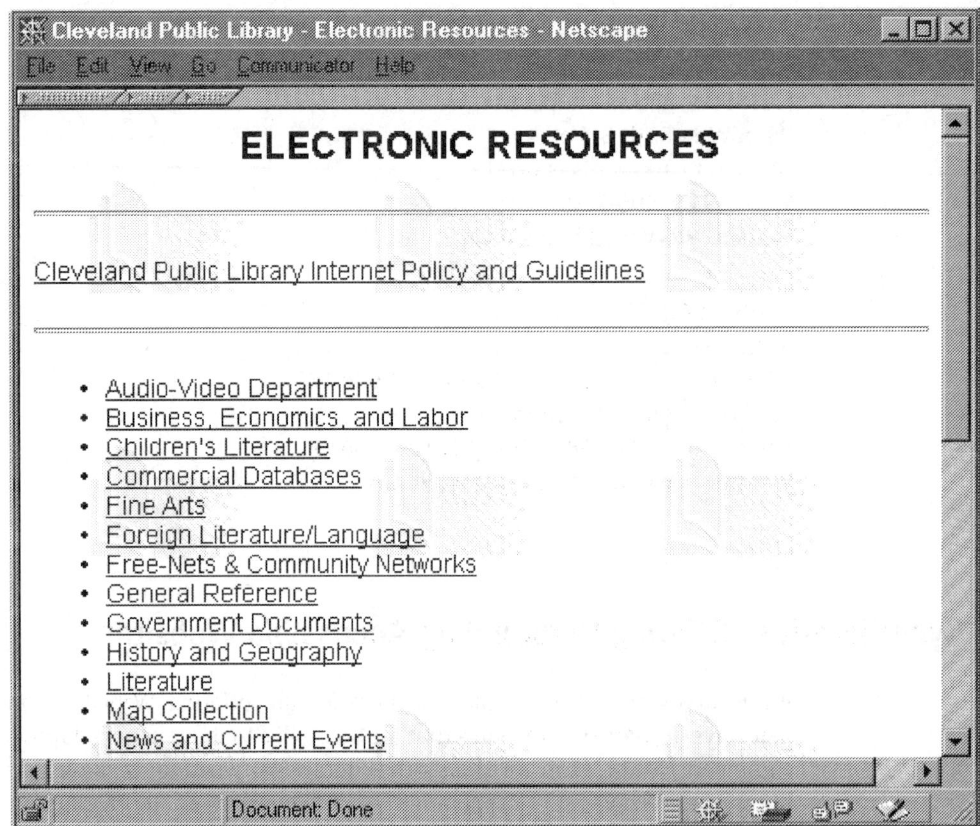

FIGURE 12-1
Electronics Resources option page

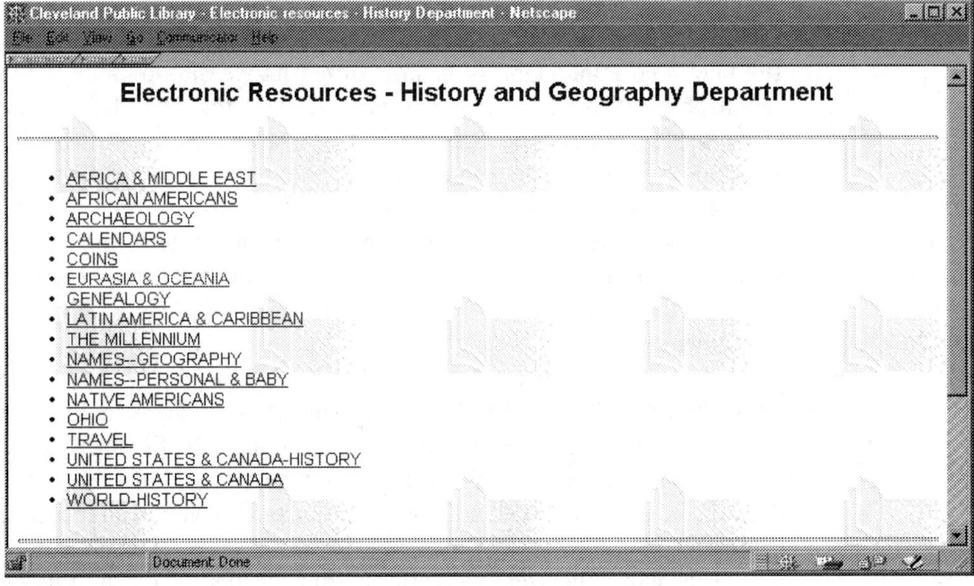

FIGURE 12-2
History and Geography Department

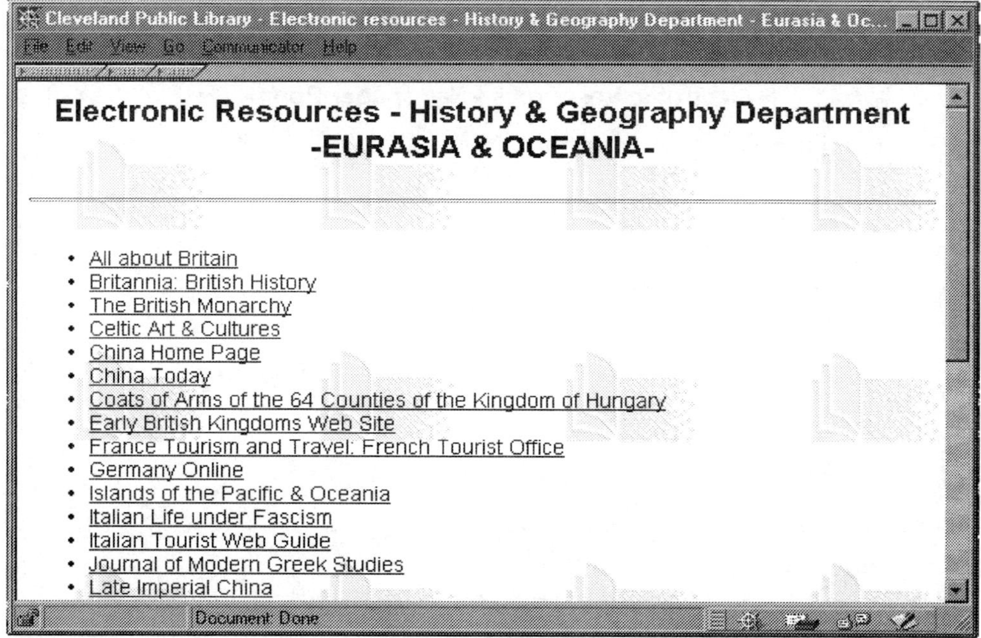

FIGURE 12-3

Eurasia & Oceania menu

Presented with two options, the user chooses Chronology: U.S.-Vietnam Relations (figure 12-4) and is able to browse until the topic being sought is found.

A visit to the Newspaper Room (shown in Figure 12-5) is as accessible to users with disabilities as a simple <PAGE DOWN> and pressing <ENTER>.

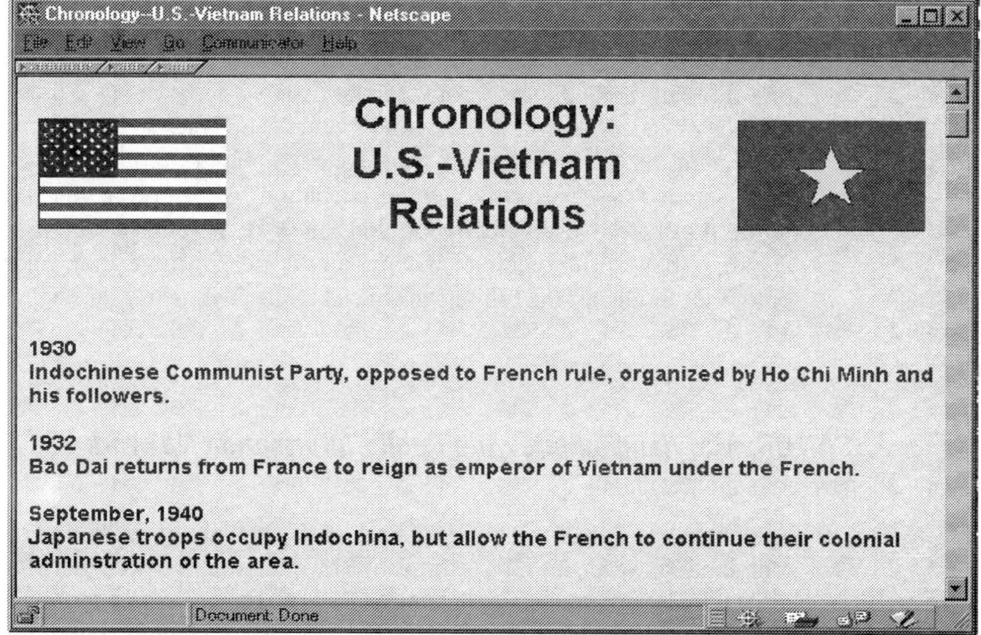

FIGURE 12-4

Vietnam news sources

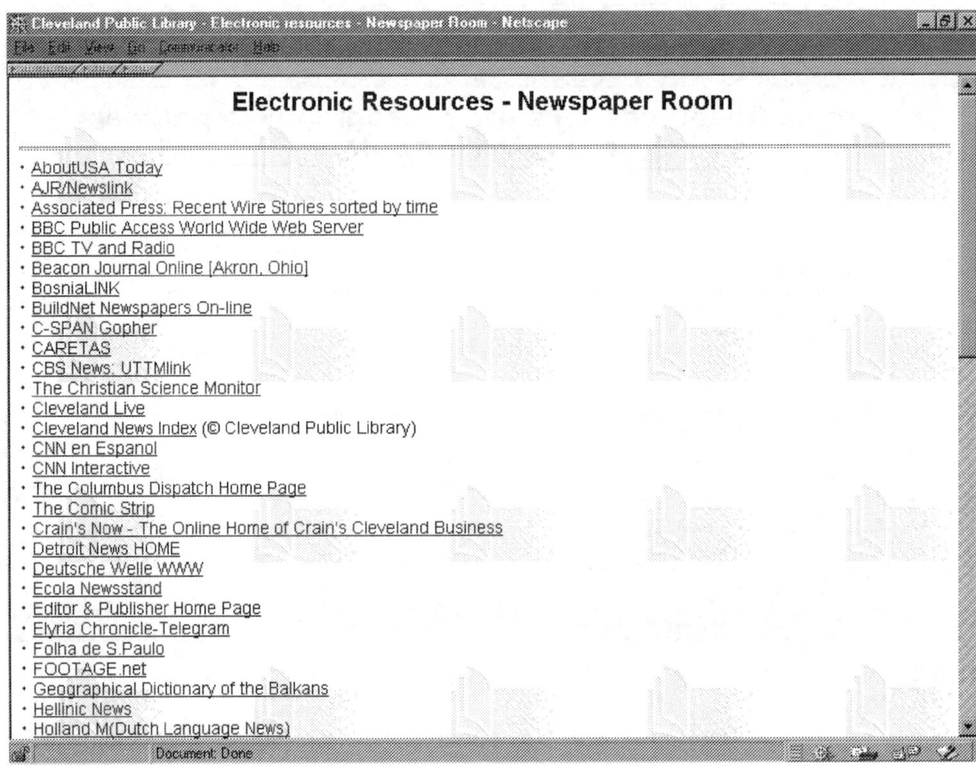

FIGURE 12-5
Newspaper Room display

Using computers to access newspapers is the only way in which people who are in need of access via Braille or large print can obtain it and virtually the only mode in which to hear the text.[3] A patron in search of articles in the *Christian Science Monitor* simply needs to scroll down until he or she locates the *Monitor* and presses <ENTER>.

Once the *Christian Science* front page is brought up (figure 12-6), a problem is foreseen, for the *Monitor* is columnized. However, you will notice that both a Text Only option and Site Map are offered. The user choosing the Text Only edition facilitates an easy read in large print, voice output, or Braille for the full screen is used to display the text (see figure 12-7).

SAILOR: Maryland's Statewide Public Information Network

<www.sailor.lib.md.us>

The home base for SAILOR is the Enoch Pratt Free Library in Baltimore, Maryland; however, SAILOR is, in reality, "owned" and "hosted" by virtually all libraries in the state. Established in 1995 to serve as a resource-sharing link between Maryland libraries, SAILOR was built by librarians (and some patrons) from all types of library communities throughout the state. Aided by the University of Maryland, 200 people worked in task

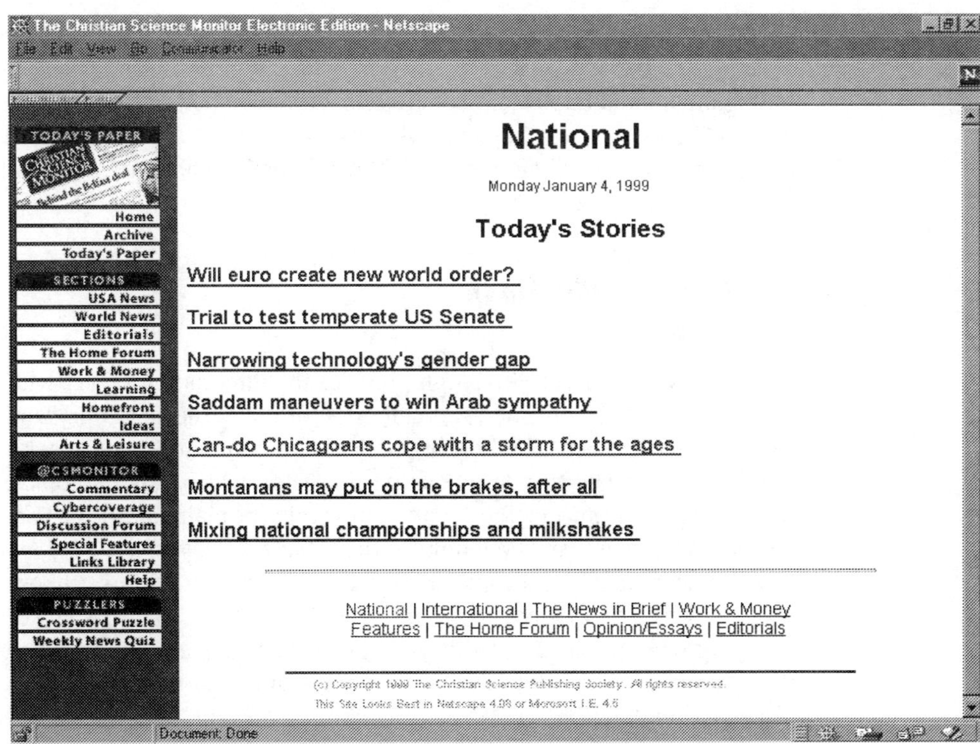

The Christian Science Monitor Electronic Edition - Netscape

TODAY'S PAPER
Home
Archive
Today's Paper
SECTIONS
USA News
World News
Editorials
The Home Forum
Work & Money
Learning
Homefront
Ideas
Arts & Leisure
@CSMONITOR
Commentary
Cybercoverage
Discussion Forum
Special Features
Links Library
Help
PUZZLERS
Crossword Puzzle
Weekly News Quiz

National

Monday January 4, 1999

Today's Stories

Will euro create new world order?

Trial to test temperate US Senate

Narrowing technology's gender gap

Saddam maneuvers to win Arab sympathy

Can-do Chicagoans cope with a storm for the ages

Montanans may put on the brakes, after all

Mixing national championships and milkshakes

National | International | The News in Brief | Work & Money
Features | The Home Forum | Opinion/Essays | Editorials

(c) Copyright 1999 The Christian Science Publishing Society. All rights reserved.
This Site Looks Best in Netscape 4.08 or Microsoft I.E. 4.0

Document: Done

FIGURE 12-6
Christian Science Monitor display

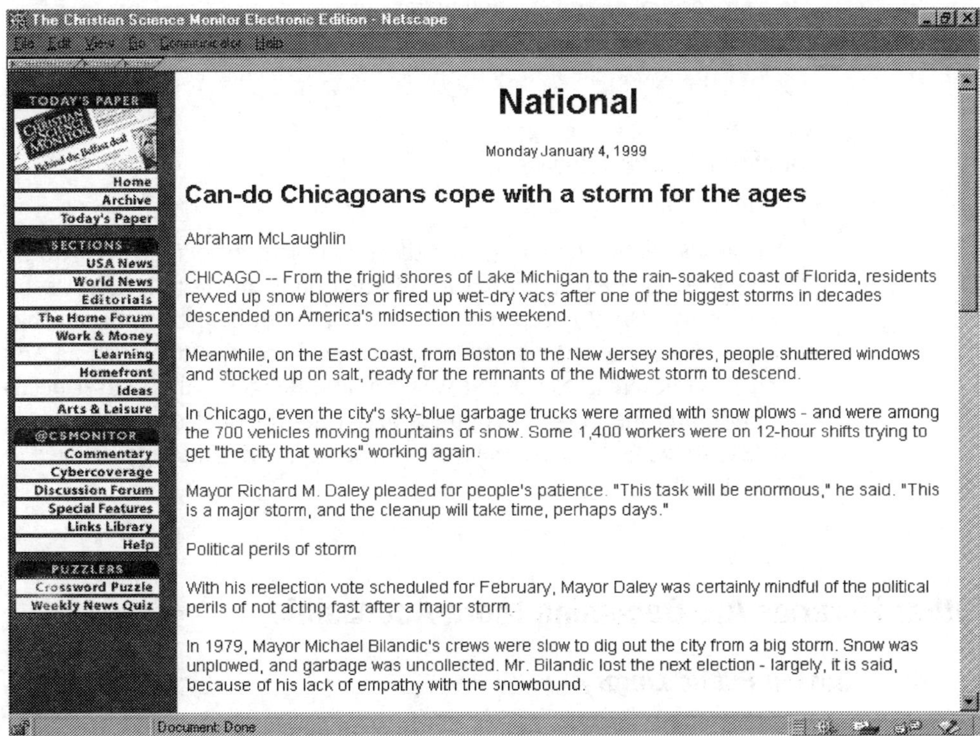

The Christian Science Monitor Electronic Edition - Netscape

National

Monday January 4, 1999

Can-do Chicagoans cope with a storm for the ages

Abraham McLaughlin

CHICAGO -- From the frigid shores of Lake Michigan to the rain-soaked coast of Florida, residents revved up snow blowers or fired up wet-dry vacs after one of the biggest storms in decades descended on America's midsection this weekend.

Meanwhile, on the East Coast, from Boston to the New Jersey shores, people shuttered windows and stocked up on salt, ready for the remnants of the Midwest storm to descend.

In Chicago, even the city's sky-blue garbage trucks were armed with snow plows - and were among the 700 vehicles moving mountains of snow. Some 1,400 workers were on 12-hour shifts trying to get "the city that works" working again.

Mayor Richard M. Daley pleaded for people's patience. "This task will be enormous," he said. "This is a major storm, and the cleanup will take time, perhaps days."

Political perils of storm

With his reelection vote scheduled for February, Mayor Daley was certainly mindful of the political perils of not acting fast after a major storm.

In 1979, Mayor Michael Bilandic's crews were slow to dig out the city from a big storm. Snow was unplowed, and garbage was uncollected. Mr. Bilandic lost the next election - largely, it is said, because of his lack of empathy with the snowbound.

Document: Done

FIGURE 12-7
Christian Science Monitor article

forces to plan and implement subprojects. Currently, half of these people are among the "master trainers" who instruct fellow staff and patrons. Funds for the launch of the site were obtained from a combination of LSCA funds and state funds.

Carnegie Library of Pittsburgh

<www.clpgh.org>

The Carnegie Library of Pittsburgh provides the information seeker with one-stop access to both the print collection of the Carnegie Library and various Internet sites. The library provides the information seeker with a defined, columned "Guide to Popular Subjects," which lists the topics, followed by call numbers, the department within the main libraries where books can be found, and Web links to the subject.

Someone looking up information on acid rain would first choose subjects whose first letter is *a* (an alphabet is listed in a line that makes browsing with switch-adapted keyboards or trackballs easier), toggle to the letter <a>, depress it, and be presented with a list of subjects from "abortion" to "anxiety" to "Aztecs." Finding "acid rain," the user could choose books on the topic of acid rain and also link to Yahoo's links to sites with acid rain content; and link to EcoNet with information on EcoNet's conferences, sites, educational resources, and further links to energy resources, and sea and water links.

While the user will need an initial orientation to the Website, the ability to browse the library by subject is commendable.

Timberland Public Library

<www.timberland.lib.wa>

Timberland Public Library offers those who log on to their Website an accessible "layered" approach to informational sites. An option, Useful Internet Sites by Subject, presents the user with subjects (aligned in a vertical file to the left side of the screen) and covers topics such as Arts and Entertainment, News and Weather, and Religion. All the user needs to do is find the topic that sounds like it fits the subject wanted, press <RETURN>, and browse the topics presented, which are, again, listed in a vertical file.

Other Libraries Are Becoming More Accessible

Boston Public Library

Boston Public Library (BPL) is gearing up to add two or three accessible workstations to its special-services department. The BPL staff plans on adding Lynx to a PC currently used for scanning and printing materials via ReadingAdvantage. They are also planning to acquire a new PC that will have JAWS, Duxbury translating software, and ZoomText Xtra Level II installed on it. This will allow total access to the Internet for users who are blind or visually impaired. They also hope to add a third terminal that could have Dragon System's Naturally Speaking and other software geared to helping users with learning disabilities access the Internet.

Michigan Washtenaw County Public Library

<www.co.washtenaw.mi.us/DEPTS/LIB/LIBSPECL/HTM>

Although the service area of the Washtenaw is relatively small, the Washtenaw County Library for the Blind and Physically Handicapped strives to make its Website and building totally accessible. Through gifts from the Ann Arbor Host Lions Club, the library has purchased a Kurzweil Personal Reader, Arkenstone Reading Edge, and CCTVs.

The Website complies with accessibility guidelines and links visitors to a Book Lovers Club, Commercially Recorded Audiobooks, the NLS catalog, and other Websites relating to blindness and visual impairments.

Lee County Library, Florida

Although the Lee County Library System does not have an Internet connection site for its patrons, the library is serving its population of persons with disabilities with assistive and adaptive technology. Plans were developed based on surveys completed by the community and comments made during public hearings. The library has over the years used local and LSCA monies to acquire items such as magnifiers, CCTVs, pocket talkers, and a public-access catalog with screen-enlargement and voice-output features. When additional grant monies were received, it hired an Assistive Technology Coordinator who developed a set of simplified instructions for each device and provided ongoing training for the library's staff on how to use the devices and how to demonstrate them for patrons.

Pinellas Talking Book Library

Presently in the process of constructing a Website (the library has contracted the services of a low-vision publisher for the construction of a home page), this subregional Talking Book Center serves a population of 850,000, of which roughly 19,000 are disabled. The center's main focal point is the circulation of talking books to registered readers, but it does offer readers adaptable access to computers. The center has large-print and Braille software translating programs and printers.

Future plans include the purchase of a PC for Internet access for PwWebSpeak, JAWS, SeeBeep, HandiKeys, and Braille keyboard overlays. The center has primarily used LSCA funds for the libraries' adaptions.

Canadian National Institute for the Blind (CNIB) Library for the Blind—"A Library without Walls"

The Canadian National Institute for the Blind (CNIB) Library for the Blind has created a library without walls for qualified Canadian residents. Realizing that a vast information resource gap existed between the nonsight-impaired population and the sight-impaired population, it sought to develop solutions that would narrow the gap or completely remove it. The CNIB Library for the Blind, under the direction of Rosemary Kavanaugh, knew that technology was at least part of the solution. It was felt that it was essential to link collections and Web-based information, use Web and digital technology, and cooperate with mainstream libraries (University of Toronto and York Public Library).

The result was resource sharing through linked catalogs and a joining of Web technology and digitalization to form VISUTEXT. VISUTEXT is a "component of VISUNET: CANADA that provides full-text access to electronic and digital media materials collected and managed by the CNIB Library."[4]

Users logging onto the server at the CNIB Library for the Blind are able to access the:

1. Churcher E-Text collection: classic titles in the public domain.
2. Electronic Reference and Information Resources: encyclopedias, dictionaries, computer guides.
3. Electronic titles in the current collection.
4. World Wide Web collection.
5. Digital audio materials.

Patrons can search VISUTEXT using Boolean operators and keywords for author, title, subject, reference resources, new titles, and type of format. Patrons wishing to browse the author index are presented with an Author Alphabetized List.

Patrons wishing to browse for Internet Reference Resources can access an alphabetical listing of topics.

A Frequently Asked Questions section is divided into broad categories and offers the information seeker the opportunity to enter a question if it is not on the list. CNIB promises a quick answer from the reference staff.

A Virtual Reference Shelf, which includes encyclopedias, dictionaries, glossaries, Internet sites (an employee listing and CNIB Core Services and Contacts), is also provided as a reference resource. Anyone may access the reference materials; however, some are proprietary and may be accessed only by CNIB patrons.

Although the CNIB VISUTEXT Collection was developed by an organization dedicated to serving the blind, the format can be emulated by a public or academic library. It would not only assist those with disabilities, but would lay the groundwork for libraries in the new millennium.

A Final Word

Begin somewhere and begin now. If all you can do is purchase a set of large-print overlays, do it; if you cannot afford those, at least develop the list of accessibility features from products you have. Everyone is entitled to information and education. Do your part to help them acquire both!

Notes

1. Kelly Pierce, "The Right Stuff: How to Choose Adaptive Technology," *Computer Users Network News: Adaptive Technology for the Blind and Visually Impaired*, III 2 (March/April 1997); III 3 (May/June 1997); III 4 (July/August 1997); III 5 (September/October, 1997). Found at <www.city~net.com/vipace/friends/chicago/newslet12>.
2. Beth Fraser, "Universal Access to the Internet for People with Disabilities," *LEO: Internet Trend Watch for Libraries* 2, 9 (September 1997).
3. The NFB offers access to *U.S.A. Today, Chicago Tribune, New York Times,* and *Washington Post* via a telephone connection. Many states support local tollfree servers. For further information, contact their Website at <www.nfb.org>.
4. Rosemary Kavanaugh and Victoria Owens, "Welcome to the CNIB Library for the Blind VISUTEXT Collection" (Paper presented at the National Library Service for the Blind and Physically Handicapped Biannual Meeting, Montreal, Quebec, Canada, May 5, 1998).

APPENDIX

A

Websites Helpful for Information on Accessibility

ABLEDATA

<www.abledata.com>

Abledata is a federally funded program whose mission is to provide information on assistive technology and rehabilitative equipment from a wide variety of international resources. In addition to offering the user access to a multitude of useful links, ABLEDATA's *Assistive Technology Directory* is available for download.

ADA Technical Assistance Program

<www.public.iastate.edu/~sbilling/ada.html>

Contains the actual information on adaptive technology as it was written.

Adaptive Technology Resource Centre (ATRC)

<www.utoronto.ca/atrc>

Total resource site for information concerning access to information. Contains papers, vendor information, and reviews.

Alliance for Technology Access (ATA)

<www.atacess.org/ATResourceLibrary>

ATA has information on Web page design, and adaptive devices, and software that enhances access to the World Wide Web for people with disabilities.

American Council of the Blind (ACB)

<www.acb.org>

One of the leading membership organizations of blind and visually impaired people.

American Foundation for the Blind (AFB)

<www.igc.apc.org/afb>

A leading national resource for people who are blind or visually impaired, the organizations that serve them, and the general public.

Apple Disability Site

<www.apple.com/disability/welcome.html>

A one-stop resource for the latest information about Macintosh assistive technology and other disability related programs.

The Archimedes Project

<www.csli.stanford.edu/arch.html>

Seeks to promote equal access to information for individuals with disabilities by influencing the early design stages of tomorrow's computer-based technology.

AskERIC Virtual Library

<http://ericir.syr.edu>

Easy search tool for educational information.

Assistive Technology Funding and Systems Change Project (ATFSCP)

<www.ucpa.org/html/innovative/atfsc>

Provides training, technical assistance, and information on assistive technology funding and systems-change issues nationwide with the goal of providing advocates with the knowledge and skills to improve access to assistive-technology devices and services for individuals with disabilities.

Assistive Technology On-Line

<www.asel.udel.edu/at-online>

Solutions to assistive technology questions may be found here.

AsTeR Synthetic Speech Application

<www.cs.cornell.edu/Info/People/raman/aster/aster-toplevel.html>

AsTeR (Audio System for Technical Reading) is a computing system for rendering technical documents in audio.

Blindness Resource Center

<www.nysise.org/blind>

The New York Institute for Special Education, along with the financial support of several vendors, maintains this Website. The site has valuable links to informational resources on the subjects of universal access, low vision resources, Braille literacy, e-text libraries, research developments. The site also has links to resources for persons with physical disabilities as well as visual disabilities. An additional plus is that it offers visitors a "text-only" option, a large-print option, and a Netscape frames format.

Center for Accessible Technology
<www.el.net/CAT>

General disabilities; children and adults; product reviews; links.

Center for Applied Special Technologies (CAST)
<www.cast.org>

A nonprofit organization whose mission is to expand opportunities for people with disabilities through innovative multimedia computer technology. Developers of Bobby, a graphical Web-based program designed to help Website designers and graphic artists make their Web pages accessible by the largest number of people.

Center for Computer Assistance to the Disabled, Inc. (C-CAD)
<www.c-cad.org>

Includes links to disability sites, a computer-training catalog, and demonstration adaptive software that can be downloaded.

Center for Information Technology Accommodation (CITA)
<www.gsa.gov/coca>

CITA's resource manual is available at this site that covers policy issues on accessibility in the workplace and methods for accommodating users with disabilities.

Closed-Captioning Web
<www.captions.org>

Resources and general information regarding the closed-captioning industry, links to deafness sites.

Closing the Gap, Inc.
<www.closingthegap.com>

Corporation offering a conference on adaptive technology as well as publishing a monthly newspaper and annual resource guide to adaptive technology.

Computing Centre for People with Disabilities
<www.wmin.ac.uk/ccpd/welcome.html>

General information on computer access for persons with disabilities. Many interesting projects discussed.

Cornucopia of Internet Disability Information
<http://codi.buffalo.ed>

General directories, statistics; links to specific disability information and bulletin boards. One of the original disability gopher sites.

Council for Exceptional Child
<www.cec.sped.org>

Geared toward educators of children with learning differences.

Deaf World
<http://dww.deafworldweb.org>

Links to many Websites of interest to persons seeking information on making sites accessible to persons with hearing impairments as well as information on sign language and deaf culture.

Department of Justice
<www.usdoj.gov/crt/508/508home> and <www.disrights.org/data/doj/webaccess.text>

The Department of Justice Website offers visitors the latest information regarding amendments to existing documents such as Section 508 on access for persons with disabilities and the Americans with Disabilities Act.

Disability Action Committee for X
<http://trace.wisc.edu/world/computer_access/dacx>

Developing methods for accessing Windows applications with adaptive technology.

Disability Resources Monthly, Inc.
<www.geocites.com/~drm>

Information presented on all disabilities and issues through the dissemination of information about books, pamphlets, magazines, databases, and online services. Links to a myriad of useful links. This site was the winner of the 1999 ALA Association of Specialized and Cooperative Library Agencies/National Organization on Disability J. C. Penney NOD Award.

Electronics Industries Association and Electronics Industries Foundation

<www.eia.org/eif/toc.html>

Presents the Resource Guide for Accessible Design of Consumer Electronics.

Equal Access to Software and Information (EASI)

<www.isc.rit.edu/~easi>

Includes information on adaptive hardware and software resources, adaptive technology publications, and designing Web pages for universal design.

Florida Alliance for Assistive Services and Technology (FAAST)

<http://faast.org>

Although designed for the state of Florida, the site offers assistive tech links, brochures on assistive technology, models of accessibility, and links to national Tech Act programs.

Gallaudet Research Institute (GRI)

<www.gallaudet.edu>

Research projects in many areas involving deafness and deaf people.

HEATH Resource Center

<www.und.nodak.edu./dept/dss/heath>

Information on postsecondary education for people with disabilities; college, vo-tech, adult education, other training.

IBM Special Needs Solutions

<www.austin.ibm.com/sns/snsvision>

Information about assistive devices and software tools that make computers more accessible to people with vision, hearing, speech, mobility, and attention/memory disabilities.

Indie (The Integrated Network of Disability Information and Education)

<www.indi.ca>

Comprehensive resource for disability-related information and products with keyword searching capabilities.

Iowa Department of the Blind: Project ASSIST

<www.blind.state.ia.us/assist>

> Tutorials offered to aid users accessing Windows applications with screen readers.

Jim Lubin's disAbility Resources

<www.eskimo.com/~jlubin/disabled>

> Extremely useful resource featuring links to a wide variety of hardware, software, funding, and training Websites.

LD Online

<www.ldonline.org>

> Site covers all aspects of LD, offering resources and links.

Learning Disabilities Association of America

<www.idanati.org>

> Information, resources for parents and professionals; local, state chapter information.

Library of Congress—The National Library Service for the Blind and Physically Handicapped (NLS)

<http://lcweb.loc.gov/nls/nls.html>

> NLS administers a free library program of Braille and recorded materials circulated to eligible borrowers through a network of cooperating libraries.

Lynx-Me

<http://ugweb.cs.ualberta.ca/%7Egerald/lynx-me.cgi>

> Lynx-Me allows you to see what your Web page looks like in a text browser.

Magical Mist Creations

<www.home.earthlink.net/~mail4tdb/text>

> Tutorials in ASCII format on diskette, cassette, large print, and Braille.

Maryland Tech Assistance Program

<www.mdtap.org>

> Developed by and for the residents of Maryland, the site offers much information on access to technology as well as offering links to adaptive technology Websites. Also offers general information on definition of access and information on laws regarding accessibility.

Matrix Parent Network
<www.matrixparents.org>

Support for parents of children with learning disabilities.

Microsoft Accessibility Support
<www.microsoft.com/enable>

Instructions on using Microsoft's accessibility tools that can help remove barriers to Windows environments.

National Adult Literacy and Learning Disabilities Center (NALLDC)
<novel.nifl.gov/nalld/nalld_states.html>

Publications, hot topics, links regarding LD and adult literacy and access.

National Braille Press
<www.nbp.org>

Braille books, pamphlets, and reference cards on Internet access.

National Center for Disability Dissemination Research (NCDDR)
<www.ncddr.org>

Disseminates efforts of NCDDR-funded research projects and increases the accessibility of research outcomes for the benefit of consumers, particularly those from minority backgrounds.

National Center for Learning Disabilities (NCLD)
<www.ncld.org>

Information on all aspects of LD; resources; links.

National Center for Supercomputing Applications (NCSA)
Mosaic Access Page
<http://bucky.aa.uic.edu>

Has information on access methods by disability, access methods by operating system, and resources including list servers and funding assistive technology.

National Center to Improve Practice (NCIP)
<www.edc.org>

Promotes the effective use of technology to enhance educational outcomes for students with sensory, cognitive, physical, and social/emotional disabilities.

National Federation of the Blind (NFB)

<www.nfb.org>

The largest organization of the blind in America.

National Information Center for Children and Youth with Disabilities (NICHCY)

<www.nichcy.org>

Information on all disabilities and related issues. Offers a lot of free (or low-cost) brochures, training packets, posters on disabilities. Also offers links to conferences, regulations, training, and state resource sites.

National Institute on Disability and Rehabilitation Research (NIDRR)

<www.ncddr.org>

The NIDRR funds approximately 300 projects and programs, many with a Web presence. Links to disability statistics sites, online foundations and corporate grant programs as well as those funded by the NIDRR are included.

NTIA Grant Program

<www.ntia.gov:70/1s/grantinfo>

Help in locating grants for adaptive technology.

Omer Zak's Home Page

<www.zak.co.il>

Links to sites with information on adapted access for persons who are deaf. Also contains tips for librarians working with children who are deaf.

Orton Dyslexia Society

<www.ods.org>

Information on dyslexia research, legislation, and state chapter contacts.

PACER Center

<www.pacer.org>

General; for families of children and Pacer adults with disabilities.

Parents Educational Resource Center (PERC)

<www.perc-schwabfdn.org>

Resources by subject and type; services, publications, links.

Parents Helping Parents
<www.portal.com/~cbntmkr/php.html>

Parents of children with various disabilities, including LD and ADD.

Parents of Gifted/Learning Disabled Children
<www.geocities.com/athens/1105/gtld.html>

Information on gifted learning disabled children; parent, child, and educator support.

The Productivity Works
<www.prodworks.com>

Manufacturer of pwWebSpeak, an Internet browser that provides both a nonvisual, auditory presentation of the World Wide Web as well as a simplified visual presentation, including large-character display.

Project DO-IT (Disabilities, Opportunities, Internetworking, and Technology
<www.washington.edu/doit>

DO-IT works to increase the participation of individuals with disabilities in science, engineering, and mathematics academic programs and careers. Great access links and information on adaptive technology.

Project HIIT—Internet for the Hearing Impaired
<www.pursuit.rehab.uiuc.edu>

Information on sites and resources for persons with hearing impairments.

Rebus Institute
<www.cenatica.com/rebus>

Literacy; for adults with learning disabilities.

Recordings for the Blind and Dyslexic
<www.rfbd.org>

Information on materials on audiotape and computer disk (E-text).

Rehabilitation Engineering and Assistive Technology Society of North America (RESNA)
<www.resna.org>

Professional organization whose purpose is to develop products and standards that improve access to technology for persons with disabilities.

Roads to Learning
<www.ala.org/roads>

Hosted by the ALA, a rich resource site for information on learning disabilities.

Royal National Institute for the Blind, UK
<www.mib.org.uk>

Site with many helpful informational fact sheets, links to resources, and ongoing research projects.

Sun Microsystems' Enabling Technologies Program
<www.sun.com/tech/access/index>

Sun is "driven by the belief that designing to meet the needs of users with disabilities can improve the productivity of all users." It offers on its Website a download of the JAVA Accessibility Utilities as well as text of presentations made by professional advocates on the subject of accessibility.

Talk-Me-Thru Tutorials
<www.crl.com/~phil>

Audiocassette tutorials walk the sight impaired computer user through various computer processes.

Technology Assessment Program
<www.gallaudet.edu>

Website of a research group whose focus is eliminating barriers traditionally faced by deaf and hard-of-hearing people. Information included on TTYs and TTY modems, captioning, accessibility, telecommunications standards, and the Telecom Act of 1996.

Technology for the Deaf
<www.computel.com/~mernix/deafworld/ref/tech/tech.html>

Resource site for technological advances for persons who are deaf.

Top Dot Enterprises
<www.eskimo.com/~deamar>

Offers audiocassette tutorials on a variety of Internet topics using adaptive technology. Also offers links to adaptive technology sites. Frequently updated.

Trace Research and Development Center
<www.trace.wisc.edu>

An interdisciplinary research, development, and resource center on technology and disability. Check here for guidelines on designing accessible HTML pages, as well as for the Java Accessibility Preliminary Examination. Also downloadable access tools are available at this site.

U.S. GSA Clearinghouse on Computer Accommodations (COCA)

See Center for Information Technology Accommodation.

University of Missouri Adaptive Technology Center
<www.missouri.edu/~ccat>

Tests and evaluations of adaptive devices.

University of Toronto

See Adaptive Technology Resource Centre.

University of Waterloo Disability Site
<www.lib.uwaterloo.ca/discipline/Disability_Issues/index.html>

Guidelines and information on computer accessibility and Web page design.

University of West Virginia's ADA Document Center
<http://janweb.icdi.wvu.edu/kinder>

Depository of ADA-related documents.

WebABLE!
<www.webable.com>

The World Wide Web information repository for people with disabilities and accessibility solution providers. Provides links to many disability Websites.

WGBH, Educational Foundation
<www.wgbh.com>

WGBH takes advantage of many techniques for making a compiled Website accessible.

World Wide Web Consortium (W3C)
<www.w3.org>

An international industry consortium, the W3C was founded in 1994 to develop common protocols for the evolution of the World Wide

Web. The W3C also sponsors the Web Accessibility Initiate (WAI), which works to make Web protocols (HTML, SGML, HTTP, etc.) more accessible to people with disabilities.

The Yuri Rubinsky Insight Foundation
<www.yuri.org>

Dedicated to bringing together workers from a broad spectrum of disciplines to stimulate research and development of technologies to enhance access to information of all kinds. Also home to WebABLE!

Digital Library Sites

Many of the sites that follow may be useful for people seeking information in special media and may not be available through the National Library for the Blind and Physically Handicapped network or Recording for the Blind and Dyslexic. Sites are well designed and accessible for persons using adaptive computer technology.

Alex: A Catalog of Electronic Texts on the Internet
<www.lib.nscu.edu/staff/morgan/alex>

A catalog of 2,000 Internet-based electronic texts of public-domain titles. Boolean search queries possible.

Classics at the Online Literature Library
<www.literature.org/Works>

Popular classics by authors such as L. Frank Baum, Bram Stoker, H. G. Wells, and Lucy Maud Montgomery can be found here.

The Internet Public Library
<www.ipl.org>

The Internet Public Library (IPL) was built by librarians to create a "strong, coherent sense of place on the Internet, while ensuring that their library remains a useful and consistently innovative environment as well as fun and easy to use." It is just that. Using "tools of the library science," the IPL has a newspaper room, which hosts a multitude of electronic international newspapers; a youth room where information is sorted by subjects, including the subject "fun stuff," and a narrated story hour; an "Online serials" division with e-text journals; and an Online Text Collection of 7,000 titles that can be browsed by author, title, or Dewey Subject Classification.

Library of Congress Internet Resource Page
<www.loc.gov/global/etext/etext>

Maintained by the Library of Congress, this site offers the user a myriad of electronic links to electronic text collections, general resources, government and legal documents, poetry sites, author sites, e-text newsletters, commercial electronic bookstores, and electronic publishing and publishers. Contains links not found elsewhere.

The On-Line Books Page
<www.cs.cmu.edu/books>

The On-Line Books site offers access to more than 9,000 items, including serials and song listings. The site features categories such as "A Celebration of Women Writers," "Banned Books On-Line," and "Prize Winners On-Line." Users may request titles to be added. Sites such as this serve to expand texts that people with disabilities "read."

Project Gutenberg
<www.promo.net/org>

The goal of Project Gutenberg is to store 10,000 electronic texts that are 99.9 percent accurate in the eyes of the general reader by the year 2001. Materials are stored in Plain Vanilla ASCII (preferred format for most adaptive technology users) and are all in the public domain. Stored texts include "light literature" (such as *Alice in Wonderland, Peter Pan*); "heavy literature" (such as *Moby Dick* and *Paradise Lost)*; and "reference works" (such as *Roget's Thesaurus,* dictionaries).

The WWW Virtual Library
<www.lib.stanford.edu>

As its name implies, the WWW Virtual Library circles the globe with mirror sites on three continents. The library is searchable by subject, keyword searches, and alphabetical listings. Subject matters range from Agriculture (subcategories include grains, wine, wool) to Regional Studies (Asian studies, Pacific studies, Indigenous studies).

APPENDIX

B

Selected Vendors, Manufacturers, and Consultants

ACCESSABILITY
320 Clement Street
San Francisco, CA 94118
Phone: (415) 751-6455; (888) 322-7200
FAX: (415) 751-5262

This vendor offers a complete line of adaptive computer equipment as well as offering the purchaser the ability to choose equipment from numerous manufacturers within the product line. It also offers setup and training.

AICOM CORPORATION
5847 Glen Eagles Drive
San Jose, CA 95131
Phone: (408) 577-0370
FAX: (408) 577-0373

Items include Accent speech synthesizers and Messenger-IC, speech synthesizers for notebook and palmtop computers.

AI SQUARED
P.O. Box 669
Manchester Center, VT 05255
Phone: (802) 362-3612
FAX: (802) 362-1670
<www.aisquared.com>

ZoomText, magnification software for DOS and Windows. VisAbility, low-vision reading software.

ALVA ACCESS GROUP
5801 Christie Avenue
Suite 475
Emeryville, CA 94608
Phone: (510) 923-6280
FAX: (510) 923-6270

E-mail: access@berksys.com
<www.aagi.com>

Developers of screen-reading and magnification software for graphical computers, including outSPOKEN and inLARGE for Macintosh and outSPOKEN for Windows 3.1 and Windows 95.

AMERICAN THERMOFORM
2311 Travers Avenue
City of Commerce, CA 90040
Phone: (213) 723-9021; (800) 331-3676
FAX: (213) 728-8877

Braille 200 interpoint, KTS Braille display, Ohtsuki printer, Comet printer.

ANN MORRIS ENTERPRISES, INC.
890 Fams Court
East Meadow, NY 11554
Phone: (516) 292-9232; (800) 454-3175
FAX: (516) 292-2522
<www.webspan.net/~annmor>

Mail-order catalog of both high- and low-end assistive devices.

ARKENSTONE
555 Oakmead Parkway
Sunnyvale, CA 94086
Phone: (408) 245-5900; (800) 444-4443
FAX: (408) 328-8484
<www.arkenstone.org>

Provides reading machines and talking maps for the blind, visually impaired, and learning disabled.

ARTIC TECHNIQUES
1000 John R
Suite 108
Troy, MI 48083
Phone: (810) 588-7370
FAX: (810) 588-2650
<www.artictech.com>

Complete line of adaptive equipment for low vision and blind individuals (speech synthesizers, screen access, notetakers, large print, CCTV, and more).

BERKELEY SYSTEMS
2095 Rose Street
Berkeley, CA 94709

Phone: (510) 540-5535
FAX: (510) 883-6270
E-mail: access_list@mail.berksys.com

Makes and sells outSPOKEN screen-reading program for Macintosh, inLARGE Macintosh screen magnification, software, and outSPOKEN for Windows.

BIOLINK COMPUTER RESEARCH & DEVELOPMENT LTD.
140 West 15th Street
North Vancouver, British Columbia V7M 1R6, Canada
Phone: (604) 984-4099

Offers Protalk for Windows, screen-reading software for Windows 3.1, Windows 95, and Windows NT. Supports a large number of speech synthesizers.

BLAZIE ENGINEERING
105 East Jarretsville Road
Forest Hill, MD 21050
Phone: (410) 893-9333
FAX: (410) 836-5040
<www.blazie.com>

Products for the blind and visually impaired.

BRAILLE RESEARCH & LITERACY INC.
1245 Hancock Street, Suite #4
Quincy, MA 02169
Phone: (617) 472-5848; (800) 407-5839
FAX: (617) 472-6003
E-mail: pduran@world.std.com

Has Vocal-Eyes screen-reading software, DecTalk speech-synthesis hardware, Index Braillers, PC Braille software, ZoomText, LP-DOS and MAGic magnification software, and ARTS and Arkenstone reading systems.

CAROLYN'S
1415 57th Avenue, West
Bradenton, FL 34207
Phone: (800) 648-2266
FAX: (941) 739-5503

Items include Vocal-Eyes, JAWS, and outSPOKEN screen-reading software; inLARGE, File-Talk, LP-DOS, InFocus, ZoomText, and MAGic magnification software; speech-synthesizer hardware and software.

CONSULTANTS FOR COMMUNICATION TECHNOLOGY
508 Bellevue Terrace
Pittsburgh, PA 15202
Phone: (412) 761-6062
FAX: (412) 761-7336
E-mail: 70272.1034@compuserv.com

Manufactures a line of augmentative communication products that are PC-based.

DAEDALUS TECHNOLOGIES
2491 Vauxhall Place
Richmond, BC V6V 1Z5, Canada
Phone: (604) 270-4605; (800) 561-5570
FAX: (604) 244-8443

DaeSSY: making technology more accessible with accessible and adjustable desks, wheelchair-mounting systems for computers and communication devices, and switch-mounting with the new STEM-SYSTEM.

DON JOHNSTON
1000 North Rand Road, Building 115, P.O. Box 639
Wauconda, IL 60084
Phone: (708) 526-2682; (800) 999-4600
FAX: (708) 526-4177
<www.donjohnston.com>

An international developer of computer access, augmentative communication, and learning disabilities hardware and software. Products include Co:Writer, Write:OutLoud, Ke:nx, Blocks in Motion, and Talk:About.

DRAGON SYSTEMS, INC.
320 Nevada Street
Newton, MA 02160
Phone: (617) 965-5200; (800) 825-5897
FAX: (617) 527-0372
<www.dragonsys.com>

Sells DragonDictate-30K, a speech-recognition system making computers understand and respond to commands given by human voice.

DUXBURY SYSTEMS, INC.
270 Littleton Road, Unit 6
Westford, MA 01886-3523
Phone: (978) 692-3000
FAX: (978) 692-7912
<www.Duxburysystems.com>

A complete line of Braille translation software for DOS, Windows, Macintosh, and other systems.

ELECTRONIC SPECIALTIES
5230 Girard Avenue North
Minneapolis, MN 55430
Phone: (612) 521-0008

Custom designs computer hardware and software systems for the visually impaired. Also repairs computers and computer-access devices.

ELECTRONIC VISUAL AID SPECIALISTS (EVAS)
Box 371
Westerly, RI 02891
Phone: (800) 872-3827; (401) 596-3155
FAX: (401) 596-3979
E-mail: contact@evas.com

Products include CompuSight Computers and adaptive aids such as speech synthesizers, screen readers, Braille printers and translators, large-print software, and CCTV/reading systems.

ENABLING TECHNOLOGIES
1601 Northeast Braille Place
Jensen Beach, FL 34957
Phone: (561) 225-3687; (800) 777-3687
FAX: (561) 225-3299
<www.brailler.com>

A complete range of interpoint and single-sided Braille embossers and dedicated Braille translators with built-in speech, all designed and manufactured in the United States.

FERGUSON ENTERPRISES
R.R.1, P.O. Box 238
Manchester, SD 57353-97228
Phone: (605) 546-2366

Sells a variety of computer hardware and software products for the visually impaired. Has a large number of accessible CD-ROM titles.

FREEDOM OF SPEECH
1524 Fairfield Road, South
Minnetonka, MN 55305
Phone: (612) 544-3333
FAX: (612) 544-7799
<www.freedomofspeech.com>

Voice-recognition technology by DragonDictate and IBM VoiceType for PC environments and PowerSecretary for the Apple/Macintosh.

GUS COMMUNICATIONS
1006 Lonetree Court
Bellingham, WA 98226
Phone: (360) 715-8580
FAX: (360) 715-9633
<www.gusinc.com>

The Gus! Multimedia Speech System for Windows converts any Windows-compatible computer into a dynamic display-speech output device. Digitized and synthetic speech, unlimited pages, scanning, page linking.

GW MICRO, INC.
725 Airport North Office Park
Fort Wayne, IN 46825
Phone: (219) 489-3671
FAX: (219) 489-2608
<www.gwmicro.com>

Computer speech-output products for people who are blind or visually impaired or have a learning disability. Plus speech input for those who cannot type.

HARRIS COMMUNICATIONS
15159 Technology Drive
Eden Prairie, MN 55344
Phone: (612) 906-1180; (800) 825-6758
FAX: (612) 906-1099
<www.harris.com>

More than 1,000 different products for deaf and hard-of-hearing children and adults: assistive devices, books, videos, and software. Ask for a 100-page complimentary catalog.

HEALTH SCIENCE
418 Wall Street
Princeton, NJ 08540
Phone: (609) 924-7616

Distributor of augmentative speech-communication products, computer-access equipment, and environmental-control units.

HENTER-JOYCE
11800 31st Court North
St. Petersburg, FL 33716-1805
Phone: (727) 803-8000; WATS: (800) 336-5658

FAX: (727) 803-8001
<www.hj.com>

JAWS for Windows and DOS (screen readers); WordScholar, a product for the learning disabled; FormMate makes filling out forms easy for the visually impaired.

HUMANWARE
6245 King Road
Loomis, CA 95650
Phone: (916) 652-7253; (800) 722-3393
FAX: (916) 652-7296
<www.humanware.com>

Specializes in talking computers, Braille terminals and printers, print-enlargement systems, and other products for people who are blind, visually impaired, or learning disabled.

IBM SPECIAL NEEDS
11400 Burnet Road, Building 904/6
Austin, TX 78758
Phone: (512) 838-4893; (800) 426-4832
FAX: (512) 838-8199
<www.ibm.com>

Develops and markets assistive devices and software tools that make the computer more accessible to persons with disabilities. These solutions assist persons with vision, mobility, speech, and attention/memory disabilities.

INNOVENTIONS
5921 South Middlefield Road, Suite 102
Littleton, CO 80123-2877
Phone: (303) 797-6554; (800) 854-6554
FAX: (303) 727-4940
<www.magnicam.com/magnicam>

Magni-Cam, an inexpensive electronic magnification system, utilizes any TV or computer monitor and is available in a totally portable battery-pack system with capabilities of CCTV.

INTELLITOOLS
55 Leveroni Court, #9
Novato, CA 94949
Phone: (415) 382-5959; (800) 899-6687
FAX: (415) 382-5950
<www.intellitools.com>

Manufacturer of the award-winning IntelliKeys keyboard has been helping people with disabilities use computers for communication, learning, and productivity since 1979.

JBLISS IMAGING SYSTEMS
1975 Hamilton Avenue, Suite 6
San Jose, CA 95125
Phone: (408) 369-7600; WATS: (888) 452-5477
FAX: (408) 369-7612
<www.jbliss.com>

Offers Internet browser tools, screen-enlargement and OCR scanning devices. Also hosts tutorials on Internet access.

KURZWEIL EDUCATIONAL SYSTEMS
411 Waverly Oaks Road
Waltham, MA 02154
Phone: (617) 899-0222; (800) 894-5374
FAX: (617) 899-3167
<www.kurzweiledu.com>

Manufacturer and distributor of software products for reading disabled, blind, and low-vision individuals.

LAUREATE LEARNING SYSTEMS
110 East Spring Street
Winooski, VT 05404
Phone: (802) 655-4755; (800) 562-6801
FAX: (802) 655-4757
<www.llsys.com>

Talking software for language development, concept development, processing, and reading designed to meet the unique needs of individuals with disabilities.

LS&S GROUP
P.O. Box 673
Northbrook, IL 60065
Phone: (800) 468-4789
FAX: (847) 498-1482
<www.Issgroup.com>

A mail-order vendor offering a wide range of adaptive computer products for most disabilities.

MAXI-AIDS
42 Executive Boulevard
P.O. Box 3209
Farmingdale, NY 11735
Phone: (800) 522-6294; (516) 752-0521
FAX: (516) 752-0689
<www.maxiaids.com>

A mail-order catalog vendor offering a wide range of high- and low-tech assistive devices.

MICROSOFT
One Microsoft Way
Redmond, WA 98052-6399
Phone: (206) 703-4929
FAX: (206) 936-7329
<www.microsoft.com>

Windows 95 operating system has built-in accessibility options that make it easier for individuals with a disability to use.

MICROSYSTEMS SOFTWARE
600 Worcester Road
Framingham, MA 01701
Phone: (508) 879-9000; (800) 828-2600
FAX: (508) 879-1069
<www.handiware.com>

HandiWARE: affordable DOS and Windows software for individuals who require screen magnification, adapted access, augmentative communication, or environmental control.

MICROTALK
3039 Aubert Avenue
Louisville, KY 40206
Phone: (502) 897-5789
FAX: (502) 721-6083
<www.microtalk.com>

Markets Automatic Screen Access Program (ASAP), which allows access to software for MS-DOS and Windows.

MISSING LINK TECHNOLOGIES
7852 Quivira Road
Lenexa, KS 66216
Phone: (913) 428-9700; (800) 388-0326
FAX: (913) 428-9797
<www.mltinfo.com>

Their logo, "Opening Doors with Computing," is their mission. They will configure a turnkey computer system to suit your needs.

NORTHPORT
6025 McKinley Pl.
Shorewood, MN 55331
Phone: (612) 474-7996
FAX: (612) 474-7996

Offers adjustable height tables.

OKAY VISION-AIDE
14811 Myford Road
Tustin, CA 92680
Phone: (800) 325-4488
FAX: (714) 669-1081
<www.ovac.com>

Offers affordable personal low-vision reading systems. Using any television, the system provides 4X to 40X magnification, reverse image, true write-under capability, and large depth of field.

OPTELEC
6 Lyberty Way
Westford, MA 01886
Phone: (508) 392-0707
FAX: (508) 692-6073
<www.optelec.com>

Low-vision products, magnifiers, CCTVs.

ORCCA TECHNOLOGY
218 McDowell Road
Lexington, KY 40502
Phone: (606) 268-1635
FAX: (606) 268-1635
E-mail: orcca@mis.net
<www.orcca.com>

Offers ScanLite: visual and auditory scanning; BitTalk: three picture switches with digitized sound; adapted photography including switch-activated Polaroid camera; EZ-TV remote control; PicSwitch; colorful Zwitch Switch.

ORIGIN INSTRUMENTS
854 Greenview Drive
Grand Prairie, TX 75050
Phone: (214) 606-8740; (800) 280-3751
FAX: (214) 606-8741
<www.orin.com>

Manufacturer of the HeadMouse, SofType, and Dragger. These products replace the functionality of a standard desktop mouse and keyboard for people who cannot use their hands. They provide access to computers, off-the-shelf software, and the Internet for people with disabilities.

PDS-PERSONAL DATA SYSTEMS, INC.
100 West Rincon Avenue, Suite 103
Campbell, CA 95008
Phone: (408) 866-1126
FAX: (408) 866-1128

Products available include DecTalk speech synthesizers, PDS Scanning Utilities, Arkenstone Readers, and Braille display systems. Complete computer systems available.

POTOMAC TECHNOLOGY
One Church Street, #402
Rockville, MD 20850
Phone: (800) 433-2838

Product line includes devices for the hearing impaired.

PRENTKE-ROMICH COMPANY
1022 Heyl Road
Wooster, OH 44691
Phone: (330) 262-1984; (800) 262-1984
FAX: (330) 263-4829
<www.prentrom.com>

Prentke-Romich Company manufactures assistive devices for people with disabilities to help them achieve their highest potential. The company offers leading technology products in speech output employing a vocabulary organization system used in the field of augmentative and alternative communication.

SCHAMEX RESEARCH
19443 Superior Street
Northridge, CA 91324
Phone: (818) 772-6644
FAX: (818) 993-2944

Offers Readman, a stand-alone portable reading machine.

SHRINK WRAP COMPUTER PRODUCTS
11706 Saddle Crescent Circle
Oakton, VA 22124
Phone: (703) 620-4642

Offers consulting services for adaptive technology. Customizes computer systems for special needs. Also a certified dealer of Arkenstone, Henter-Joyce, MicroTalk, and TeleSensory products.

SIGHTED ELECTRONICS
464 Tappan Road
Northvale, NJ 07646
Phone: (201) 767-3977; (800) 666-4883
FAX: (201) 767-0612
<www.sighted.com>

Index Basic-D Braille printer for fan-folded paper. Index Everest Braille printer for separate papers.

SYNTHA-VOICE COMPUTERS
304-800 Queenston Road
Stoney Creek, ON L8G 1A7, Canada
Phone: (905) 662-0565
FAX: (905) 662-0568
<www.synthavoice.on.ca>

Access to DOS, Windows, and Windows 95 through speech, Braille, and large print.

TASH
Unit 1, 91 Station Street
Ajax, ON L1S 3H2, Canada
Phone: (905) 686-4129; (800) 463-5685
FAX: (905) 686-6895
E-mail: tashcan@aol.com

TECHNOLOGIES FOR THE VISUALLY IMPAIRED
9 Nolan Court
Hauppauge, NY 11788
Phone: (516) 724-4479
<www.tvi-web.com>

Vendor that handles the Rainbow Reading machines and a variety of adaptive technologies.

TELESENSORY SYSTEMS
520 Almanor Avenue
Sunnyvale, CA 94086-3533
Phone: (408) 616-8700; WATS: (800) 804-8004
FAX: (408) 616-8720

Develops and distributes information-access products for blind and visually impaired people, including state-of-the-art Braille displays, Windows and DOS access software, the OsCaR scanning system, Braille and speech notetakers, and Braille embossers.

UNIVERSAL LOW VISION AIDS, INC.
1550 College Hill Drive
Columbus, OH 43221-4317
Phone: (800) 369-0347; (614) 486-0098
FAX: (614) 486-1043

Distributes Arkenstone and Blazie Engineering products, a variety of screen readers, speech synthesizers, and screen-enlarging software, including ZoomText and LP-DOS.

VOILA TECHNOLOGY
54 Castle Road
Rochester, NY 14623
Phone: (716) 321-1451
FAX: (716) 321-1451

Voice input/output systems for people with print disabilities. These systems include Verbal-Ease, Kurzweil VOICE, IBM VoiceType, and DragonDictate.

WESTEST ENGINEERING
1470 North Main Street
Bountiful, UT 84010-5910
Phone: (801) 298-7100
FAX: (801) 292-7379
<www.darci.org>

DARCI products: DARCI TOO, a universal computer-access device, and the DARCI cards, PCMCIA-based computer access.

WILLIAMS SOUND
10399 West 70th Street
Eden Prairie, MN 55344
Phone: (612) 943-2252; (800) 328-6190
FAX: (612) 943-2174

Assistive-listening products, ADA-compliant products, large- and small-area FM systems, TV amplifiers, amplified telephones, personal amplifiers.

WORDS +
40015 Sierra Highway, Building B-145
Palmdale, CA 93550
Phone: (805) 266-8500; (800) 869-8521
FAX: (805) 266-8969
E-mail: WordsPls@aol.com

Leaders in the field of augmentative and alternative communication. Provides the latest technology, pictographic and text language-based AAC products for Windows application.

XEROX IMAGING SYSTEMS
9 Centennial Drive
Peabody, MA 01960
Phone: (508) 977-2000; (800) 248-6550
FAX: (508) 977-2437
<www.xerox.com/xis>

Provides adaptive-technology products for individuals who are blind, visually impaired, and dyslexic. Products include The Reading Edge, AdvantEdge, and BookWise.

ZYGO INDUSTRIES
P.O. Box 1008
Portland, OR 97207
Phone: (503) 684-6006; (800) 234-6006
FAX: (503) 684-6011

Communication systems, environmental controls, and technology for cognitively impaired individuals.

APPENDIX

C

Special Libraries with Adaptive Technology Programs

The following libraries represent a cross section of those making efforts to ensure that all members of the community they serve are able to access information. These libraries were brought to the attention of the author in various ways, but mainly through word of mouth—people and patrons who justifiably have something good to say about these institutions. With one exception, these institutions did not have a "fairy godmother" wave a magic wand to make their buildings and computer systems accessible. They did it by planning, creative budgeting, and hard work.

Librarians were asked various questions, such as the equipment that is available, the policies for using the equipment, the costs of the equipment, the source of their funding, the staff training that is required, and the usage by the community. A staff name was also provided for those who may wish to contact someone for advice.

All of the libraries are not at the same level of access to information and are included to illlustrate that any organization can start the process and attain ongoing success.

COLLEGE CENTER for LIBRARY AUTOMATION (CCLA)
1238 Blountstown Highway
Tallahassee, Florida 32304
Voice: (850) 922-6044
Website: <www.ccla.lib.fl.us>

Background: CCLA delivers Library Information Network for Community Colleges (LINCC) to the 28 community colleges in Florida. The center does not serve the user directly, but rather it trains the library staff, who are then able to assist the end users.

CCLA developed the LINCC Assistive Technology Workstation to provide independent access to services of the community college library. One workstation is provided at each dedicated site in Florida for a total of 60 workstations in the state.

Population Served: The population is a publicly funded academic one in both rural and suburban settings. One million students and teachers are served by these libraries.

Adaptive Equipment: CCLA maintains a large-print monitor, screen reading software, and large print keytops. It uses a standard dot matrix printer.

Do Procedures Allow for the Downloading of Information onto Disk? No.

Usage: Unknown.

Expenditures: $5,000.

Funding Source: Special allocation from funding agency.

Development Time: One year.

Staff Training Module: Two hours were needed to train staff and all staff were trained. Facilitated by a training manual. See "Other Comments" that follow.

Website Design: The LINCC Website, LINCCWEB, was specifically designed to be used by both text-only browsers and graphical browsers. It can be successfully accessed by screen-reading software.

Other Comments: Each workstation is provided with a two-volume set of documentation, *LINCC Assistive Technology Workstation User Guide,* to introduce the library's public service staff to the workstation's basic functionality. The guide includes a 20-minute introductory video and is supplemented by vendor documentation and other materials for troubleshooting and maintenance.

Contact: Amy Chapman, Administrative Information Specialist, CCLA.

SAN JOSE STATE UNIVERSITY LIBRARY (SJSUL)
One Washington Square
San Jose, California 95192-0028
Voice: (408) 924-2818
Library Website: <www.library.sjsu.edu>
Disability Resource Center (DRC) Website: <www.drc.sjsu.edu>
City of San Jose Website that cites disability access design standards: <www.ci.sanjose.ca.us/oaacc/disacces>

Background: San Jose State University is located in one of the few cities that have established "Disability Access Design Standards" for its World Wide Web pages with the hopes that citizens with disabilities would be able to navigate freely throughout the Net. The university also incorporates a Disability Resource Center (DRC) that operates a High-Tech Center on the first floor of the library where an additional eight accessible workstations are located.

Population Served: Public institution in urban setting. Total students registered is 26,000, of which approximately 1,250 students are disabled.

Adaptive Equipment: The library maintains ten large-print display PCs (five Web-based), one CCTV, nine PCs with screen-reader modifications (five

Web-based), four large-print/Braille keytops, one OCR reader. Alternate keyboards and mouse adaptions are on order. The DRC also supports a Braille printer, adapted keyboards, OCR machines, voice-recognition technology.

Do Procedures Allow for the Downloading of Information onto Disk? Yes.

Usage: Ten to twenty students a week; maybe more as students activate adaptions as needed.

Expenditures: Approximately $1,500 per station at the SJSUL; $400,000 over five years for the DRC.

Funding Source: SJSUL: 5 percent Special Allocation, 95 percent General Operating Fund; DRC collaborative effort from the Chief Information Officer, the Director of the DRC, and the President's Office.

Development Time: The SJSUL has been acquiring and retiring equipment for ten years; the DRC is working with a five-year plan.

Staff Training Module: Twenty-five percent of service staff are trained in use of adaptive equipment. Training time is two hours.

Website Design: Launched in May of 1998. The site follows the Universal Design Standards of Trace Institute. The site carries the NCAM logo.

Contacts: Library: Donna Pontau, Library Liaison to Users with Disabilities. DRC: Eric Christienson.

SAN FRANCISCO PUBLIC LIBRARY
Blind Services Center and Deaf Services Center
100 Larken Street
Civic Center
San Francisco, California 94102
Voice: (415) 557-4253; TTD: (415) 557-4433
Website: <www.sfpl.lib.ca.us>

Background: The San Francisco Public Library houses both a Blind Services Center (which is a subregional library of the National Library Service (NLS) for the Blind and Physically Handicapped) and a Deaf Services Center. The Blind Services Center houses a collection of popular reading materials on tape and the largest assembly of print-accessibility equipment in the United States. The Deaf Services Center was established in 1977 and relocated to the main library in 1996. It is considered the "ideal deaf library," for it is located in a room without windows (preventing glare). Additionally, shelves are low and tables are round so users who communicate with sign language or speech reading can see one another comfortably.

The library also houses a Resource Collection for Learning Differences, believed to be the largest of its kind in the United States. It is located on the third floor near the reference desk for the general collections. A librarian is devoted to developing collections and services for people with learning disabilities and ADD/ADHD. Adult new reader material is located nearby.

A 1994 report to help the library identify problems that people with learning disabilities (LD) have in using its services and to shape technology-based solutions, *Technology to Improve the Accessibility of the New San Francisco Main Library for Learning Disabled Users,* was written by John Anton and Jerome Elkind of the Lexia Institute, Greg Miller of Stanford University, and Marshall Raskind of the Marianne Frostig Center, all experts in technology for people with LD. It was funded by the Charles and Helen Schwab Foundation.

Population Served: A public library serving the greater San Francisco area.

Adaptive Equipment: The library has 33 PCs with large-print software modifications, three CCTVs, 33 PCs with screen-reading devices, one PC with a refreshable Braille display and keytops, 11 laser jet printers with large-print fonts, one Braille printer, 11 OCR readers and closed-captioned decoders. Additionally, several of the library's meeting rooms are equipped with listening devices that make communication easier for the hearing impaired.

There also are 13 "added access terminals" or "ADA OPACS" available for using the online catalog and accessing the Internet through a non-graphical browser. As of early 1999, the added access terminals have ZoomText and Vocal Eyes programs installed. These terminals may be used by anyone, but priority is given to persons with disabilities.

As a result of the above-mentioned 1994 technology report on learning disabilities, "enhanced workstations" were installed in selected small study rooms throughout the library. These include various programs that can be used to magnify text; hear text spoken aloud from a screen; scan in materials that are then spoken aloud, printed out, or copied to disk; and write documents and control the computer by dictating into a microphone.

Enhanced workstations accommodate people with disabilities in addition to those with learning disabilities. Their use is restricted to people with disabilities who have a valid San Francisco Public Library card and check in at the paging desk. The adaptive technology technician employed by the library conducts interviews with prospective users and registers them.

Cost: When originally installed, the enhanced workstations cost approximately $15,000 each. Prices for both hardware and software have dropped precipitously, making comparable setups much less expensive, estimated to be in the $5,000 to $6,000 range. Software has also been improved in terms of ease of use and, where necessary, training time required.

Usage: Because the equipment is distributed throughout the building, it is impossible to determine.

Expenditures: Unable to estimate, for much of the expenditures for the centers came from a grant from the Charles Schwab Foundation when the main library was being built.

Funding Source: LSCA, Library Foundation Grant, the Charles and Helen Schwab Foundation.

Development Time: Six years. Updates and improvements ongoing.

Staff Training Module: Few staff are actually trained; the position of adaptive technology technician has been established specifically for training staff and patrons.

Other Comments: Talking signs are used throughout the building to help guide visitors unable to read signs to their destination. The Deaf Services staff has bilingual members who are available to act as interpreters throughout the building. The Deaf Services Center also provides interpreter services or real-time captioning for library programs and events, when requested in advance.

The Resource Collection for Learning Differences is part of a service that includes a librarian and occasional programs and speakers on learning disabilities and related topics through the Schwab Foundation for Learning.

Contacts: Martin Magid, Head, Blind Services Center; and Marti Goddard, Head, Deaf Services Center; Marilyn Dong, Librarian, Resource Collection for Learning Differences.

SEATTLE PUBLIC LIBRARY
Library Equal Access Program (LEAP)
1000 4th Avenue
Seattle, Washington 98104
Voice: (206) 386-4690
Website: <www.spl.org>

Background: LEAP was established to make the Seattle Public Library a valuable resource for the visually impaired. Through the use of adaptive equipment, print-disabled individuals can now benefit from the library's collection of more than 1,000,000 items otherwise not available in large print, Braille, or sound recordings.

Population Served: A public library serving a large metropolitan area. In 1996 in the city of Seattle, an estimated 534,732 people used the library.

Adaptive Equipment: In the Seattle Public Library, LEAP provides three oversized monitors, five PCs with large-print screens and keyboard modifications, a CCTV, an OCR reading machine, a refreshable Braille display, two laser jet printers with large-print fonts, and a Braille printer.

Usage: Approximately 140 patrons use the equipment (40 are very active users).

Expenditures: $50,000.

Funding Source: Combination of General Operating Funds, Friends Group, LSTA grants and special grants.

Development Time: Seven years.

Staff Training Module: Two hours; only 2 percent of library staff is fully trained, the head of LEAP.

Website Design: By Cleo Brooks, the LEAP Website is straight text (no frills), which means that it can easily be read with accessible resources.

Other Comments: LEAP provides wonderful promotional brochures for its site and services. The LEAP guide (in large print) states what resources are available as well as what services are provided. LEAP offers orientation to the library and escorts within the library. The library provides assistive-listening devices for use within the library and will provide interpreters for special programs. Additionally, a "looped" meeting room is available for group events.

Contact: Cleo Brooks, Head, LEAP.

JOHNSON COUNTY LIBRARY
9875 West 87th Street
Overland Park, Kansas 66212
Voice: (913) 495-2400
Website: <www.jcl.lib.ks.us>

Background: With the passage of the ADA, the staff of the Johnson County Library began an intensive program of building modification, new-equipment acquisition, staff education, and community-awareness promotion. In October of 1996, the library celebrated its first-ever Disabilities Awareness Month. The staff realize their work is still not complete and look to improve access.

Population Served: A suburban public library serving a population of 334,200.

Adaptive Equipment: The Johnson County Library provides patrons with 12 oversize monitors, with large-print software modifications, one CCTV, and an OCR scanner. Additionally, one PC has a screen reader with speech output. The library had several telephone devices for the deaf (TDDs) installed and had assistive-listening devices installed in public meeting rooms. Budgeted for fiscal year 1999 are large-print/Braille keytops, a Braille printer, and keyboard and mouse adaptions.

Do Procedures Allow for the Downloading of Information onto Disk? Yes.

Usage: More than ten people weekly.

Expenditures: $60,000.

Funding Source: Special allocation from parent agency.

Development Time: Two years.

Staff Training Module: Two hours; all staff are trained in using the equipment.

Website Design: In-house, with links to other ADA/accessibility sites.

Other Comments: Adaptions at the Johnson County Library were added at the suggestions of the ADA committee. The committee and the library hope to find funds to expand access services. The library also has 25 handheld and table magnifiers, which are extremely helpful for persons with declining vision who are not psychologically ready for high-tech devices. The ADA committee prepared handouts on equipment use and in 1996 completely revised all marketing materials to better explain the library's services to the disabled. The committee additionally formed a community advisory group and surveyed the public to see what improvements could be made.

Contact: Kent Oliver, Branch Services Manager.

FAIRFAX COUNTY LIBRARY
Access Services
12000 Government Center Parkway, Suite 123
Fairfax, Virginia 22035-0012
Voice: (702) 324-8380; TTY: (703) 324-8635
Website: <www.co.fairfax.va.us/library>

Background: Access Services has just moved to a new centrally located facility so it will be easier for people with disabilities to visit. The Fairfax County Library System, in its commitment to making services accessible to everyone, established Access Services with emphasis on Services for People Who Are Blind or Visually Impaired, Services for People Who Are Deaf or Hard of Hearing, Services for People Who Are Homebound, and For People with Any Disability and Family, Friends, and Caregivers.

Population Served: A suburban public library serving a population of 899,650.

Adaptive Equipment: Four oversize monitors, five PCs with large-print software modifications, six PCs with screen-reading software, one PC with a refreshable Braille display, two large-print/Braille keytops, two laser printers, one Braille printer, three OCR readers, and one ergonomic workstation.

Usage: In addition to patron usage of equipment, demonstrations are given for people who are thinking about using the technology. When a series on Southern literature was presented, special services such as captioning, recorded books, and audio enhancement were offered. Six percent of the 800 who attended specifically asked for assistive-listening devices. It was not determined how many used the closed-captioning display, the large-print, or the recorded versions of the books discussed.

Expenditures: $300,000.

Funding Source: A combined effort of special allocations from the parent agency, small gifts from patrons and Lions groups, LSCA, LSTA grants, and other grants.

Development Time: Ten years.

Staff Training Module: All staff know how to use the equipment and training is ongoing.

Website Design: Developed by the Fairfax County Network Coordinator, the Website is totally accessible with adaptive technology and rightfully displays the "Bobby Approved" symbol.

Other Comments: The library describes users of some of its adaptive technology: a father of a blind student who uses the Braille printer to print tests forms for his son, and a visually impaired student who uses CD-ROM material displayed in large print on a large-screen monitor.

Glossary

Accessible Web design A design that ascribes to universal design principles that seek to eliminate or reduce barriers, including those that affect people with disabilities or whose economics prohibit upgrades of computer equipment.

Accommodation An adjustment to make facilities, programs, and services accessible to persons with disabilities.

Adaptive technology A wide variety of electronic items that enable an even wider variety of people with disabilities to live independently. Many of the devices are based on computer technology.

Address A string of characters used in cyberspace that allows users to identify themselves.

Alt attribute The HTML code that when combined with graphical tags provides a vehicle for alternative text for graphical elements.

American Sign Language (ASL) A sign-language system for the deaf that uses specific hand gestures in relation to the upper body for communication purposes.

Applet A computer program that is launched from within another application.

ASCII American Standard Code for Information Interchange. A standard set of characters (128) used by computers. This "universal language" allows adaptive technology to work.

Auxiliary aids and services According to the Americans with Disabilities Act, this includes securing qualified interpreters or other devices to make aurally delivered materials accessible to persons with hearing impairments; or securing readers, taped texts, or devices to deliver print materials to persons with visual impairments. Frequently, auxiliary aids include modified equipment or devices.

Board An integrated circuit board that plugs into a slot (open space) in the computer.

Boot To turn on or restart a computer.

Braille A writing system using raised dots in patterns (cells) that represent the standard text alphabet.

Braille embosser/printer A device that produces Braille mechanically or electronically; some are driven by a PC.

Browser Software that allows the user to access the World Wide Web. Browsers may be graphical or text-based. Text-based browsers do not display graphics or sound clips.

Captioned film, video Text description of spoken script that allows people who are deaf to fully enjoy the presentation.

Card *See* Board

Carriage length The maximum number of characters on a line; it varies with the type of print used.

Closed captioning A method by which American Sign Language translations are either broadcast live to television sets with captioning decoders or laid down on a track of videotape recordings. This allows the hearing impaired or deaf person to "hear" the dialogue as it is being spoken.

Closed-circuit displays (CCDs) A closed-circuit system that enlarges almost any item placed on its viewing tray.

Closed-circuit TV (CCTV) A system consisting of a television camera that takes a picture of an item and projects the enlarged display on a monitor.

Computer Braille A Braille code developed by the Braille Authority of North America (BANA) that added items primarily used in computer communications (example: the backslash \ or the vertical bar |).

Digital format Computer-formatted data or information. Digitized information may be text, sound, or graphical.

Download The process that transfers computer files from one source to another.

Expanded keyboard A keyboard that has keys and spaces between individual keys. This configuration enables a person with limited dexterity to accurately input information into the computer.

File Transfer Protocol (FTP) The Internet tool that allows the user to copy files from one computer to another over the Internet.

Grade-II Braille The accepted form of written Braille communication that consists of the Braille alphabet, numbers, and punctuation marks in an abbreviated format. Common words and letter contractions are reduced to a type of shorthand that eliminates the need to spell out words such as *with* or *the* and eliminates the tedium of printing and reading a cell for every letter.

Graphical User Interface (GUI) Program interface that allows the user to view a character-based format as a graphical presentation.

HTML Hypertext Markup Language used to create World Wide Web pages.

HTML validation Process that analyzes HTML documents in comparison to rules identifying errors.

Hyperlink Highlighted word or graphic on a Web page that when selected allows the user to travel to another part of the document or another Web location.

Hypertext The format that allows the user to link a word or phrase in one document to a related document anywhere in the Web.

Image map Picture of a graphic on a Web page in which hyperlinks are embedded.

Internet Computer network that allows individual computers to connect to computer systems worldwide.

Java Programming language used to create programs or applets that work with browsers to explore the World Wide Web and allow features such as animation to be added.

Joystick A device equipped with a single control lever that tilts in different directions to allow individuals with limited dexterity to input information into a computer.

Keyguard A template that fits over the keyboard and keys. The holes in the cover correspond to each key on the keyboard and help persons with limited dexterity to correctly isolate the key they wish to depress.

Large monitor Any monitor that is larger than 17 inches. It enables the user to enlarge print without losing continuity.

Large print A print type that is larger than 13.9 printer's points or about 4.5 millimeters from the top of the ascenders to the bottom of the descenders in lowercase.

Large-print screen displays Available in many formats, such as a simple magnifier, closed-circuit television type technology, or an enlarged screen.

Link Any connection between two files or computers.

Lynx A text-based browser that allows users to access information on the Internet. Often used by persons with adaptive equipment or older computer equipment.

Membrane keyboard A flat keyboard with programmable keys. This keyboard allows persons with limited and varied strength to input information into a computer. If, for instance, the user has more strength in his or her thumbs and little fingers, frequently used letters such as <a> and <s> and function keys such as <ENTER> and <SPACE> would be programmed within the reach of these appendages.

Menu A programming technique that lists choices that are available to the user.

Micro-keyboard (mini) A keyboard on which the keys are grouped together as closely as possible so users whose fingers cannot flex over a standard keyboard can access the entire keyboard. The micro-keyboard is very often the size of a pocket calculator.

Mouthstick A mouthpiece that serves as a finger to control a computer or other device. The user is able manipulate the controls using this small device.

OCR scanner A computer-based optical character recognition system that translates material into an electronic format that can then be stored and accessed via a computer monitor, a printer, or an adapted device such as a speech synthesizer or a Braille display.

Paperless Braille display A device that translates the ASCII notations it sees to small pins that are raised or lowered electronically to form different Braille characters. No hard copy is made.

Phoneme Smallest measurement of speech sound. These elementary speech sounds are represented by the letters of the alphabet. In the English alphabet, however, some phonemes are represented by a combination of letters (*th* or *sh*) and some letters represent more than one phoneme (c, g, o).

Phonological awareness The ability to attend to the phonological or sound structure of language and to be aware of words, syllables, and phonemes.

PPP (Point to Point Protocol) An interface used with a modem to connect to the Internet.

Print awareness (orthographic awareness) An awareness of how print works and how it looks. Print is made up of letters, letters correspond to sounds and words, and text in the English language is read from left to right across the page.

Refreshable Braille *See* Paperless Braille display

Screen reader A software program used with a speech synthesizer to properly interpret and read text.

SLIP (Serial Line Interface Protocol) An interface used with a modem to connect to the Internet.

Speech synthesizer A device that converts text characters into artificial speech using a standard pronunciation rule for speech.

Switch interface A software or hardware device that acts as a link between the switch and the computer.

Switches Used in conjunction with a hardware or software device to provide input to the computers or assistive devices such as battery-operated wheelchairs. A variety of types of switches, including pressure switches, pneumatic switches, and voice-activated switches, are available.

Tag HTML code that designates the structure and the format of Web pages.

Telecommunication Devices for the Deaf (TDD) or **Teletypewriters (TTYs or TTs)** Terms often used interchangeably to describe a telephone that allows the user to type a message rather than use speech.

Touch screen An input device that allows access to a computer by touching the screen. These are widely used commercially at retail outlets and banks.

Trackball Resembles and functions like a mouse but does not have a contoured housing that fits neatly into a typical hand. Buttons on the trackball emulate the clicks of a mouse. Trackballs are easier to use for persons who cannot manipulate a mouse.

Universal design Designing programs, services, tools, and facilities so that they are usable without modification by the widest range of users, taking into account the users' abilities and disabilities.

URL (Universal Resource Locator) Address used to locate a specific resource on the Internet.

Voice recognition A device that is programmed to recognize the voice of the user and execute the voice commands made by the user.

Web Accessibility Initiative (WAI) Founded in 1997 to promote and achieve Web functionality for people with disabilities. The International Program Office (IPO) of the World Wide Web is responsible for developing software protocols and technologies, creating guidelines for their use, educating the industry, and coordinating research and development.

Web page A document that could either be graphic- or text-based, found on the World Wide Web.

World Wide Web (WWW, W3, or Web) Hypertext and multimedia gateway to the Internet.

World Wide Web Consortium (W3C) Founded in 1994 to develop common standards for the evolution of the WWW. Membership is international.

Bibliography and Reading Resources

Access 20/20. "Designing an Accessible Web Page." Developers Page. Available at <www.access2020/cpm/develop.html>.

Arnold, David. "Speech Recognition Application and Limitations for Motor Impaired." Paper presented by David Arnold of Olive Tree Software at the 1998 CSUN Conference sponsored by California State University, Northridge, Center on Disabilities, March 1998. Available at <www.dinf.org/csun_98/csun98>.

Banks, Richard, and Norman Combs. "Libraries without Walls." Paper presented by Banks and Combs, Project EASI at the 1996 CSUN Conference sponsored by California State University, Northridge, Center on Disabilities, March 1996. Available at <www.rit.edu/~easi/lib/csun96bc>.

Becker, Stig, et al. "CESAR Comparative Evaluation of Screen Alternatives for Reading." *Closing the Gap* (June/July 1997): 1–11.

Bergman, Eric, and Earl Johnson. "Towards Accessible Human-Computer Interaction." *Advances in Human-Computer Interaction.* Vol. 5. Edited by Jakob Nielson. Norwood, N.J.: Ablex, 1995.

Berliss, J. R. *Checklists for Making Library Automation Accessible to People with Disabilities.* Madison: Wisc.: Trace R&D Center, 1992.

Cantor, Alan. "Avoiding the Mousetrap: An Evaluation of Keyboard-Only Access to Windows." Paper presented at the 1998 CSUN Conference sponsored by California State University, Northridge, Center on Disabilities, March 1998. Available at <www.dinf.org/csun_98>.

———"The AD-A-P-T-A-B-L-E Approach: Planning Accessible Libraries." *Information Technology and Disabilities* 2 (4). Available at <www.rit.edu/~easi/itd/itdv02n4/article2>.

Center for Applied Special Technology. "BOBBY." Peabody, Mass., 1997. Available at <www.cast.org/bobby/understand>.

Chalfen, Daniel. "Usability of Information and the WWW." Los Angeles: UCLA. Available at <www.dcp.ucla.edu/patrick/webusel>.

Cirillo, Susan, and Robert E. Danford. *Library Buildings, Equipment, and the ADA.* Chicago: American Library Association, 1996.

Clearing House on Computer Accommodation (COCA). "Overview of Accommodation." Section 3 of *COCA Handbook Managing Information Resources* (September 1994). Available at <www.itpolicy.gsa.gov/coca/sec_3>.

Conger, Dean, and Nik Corbis. "Microsoft NetMeeting and the Role of Internet Conferencing for Deaf and Hard-of-Hearing Users." Press Release. Microsoft, "Legal Notices," February 1998. Found at <www.microsoft.com/enable>.

Cook, Rick. "Best Practices: Web Design for Everyone Including the Disabled." Netscape Enterprise Developer, August 1996. Found at <www.netscapeworld.com/netscapeworld>.

Cunningham, Carmela, and Norman Coombs. *Information Access and Adaptive Technology.* Phoenix: American Council on Education and Oryx Press, 1997.

DeWitt, John C., and Markku Hakkinen. "Surfing the Web with pwWebSpeak." Paper presented for DeWitt & Associates, Productivity Works, New Jersey at the 1998 CSUN Conference sponsored by California State University, Northridge, Center on Disabilities, March 19, 1998.

Dienes-Jones, Courtney, and Connie Van Fleet. *Preparing Staff to Serve Patrons with Disabilities: A How-to-Do-It Manual for Librarians.* New York: Neil-Schuman, 1995.

Dixon, Judith. "Leveling the Road Ahead: Guidelines for the Creating of WWW Pages Accessible to Blind and Visually Handicapped Users." *Library Hi-Tech* 53 (1996): 65–68.

DO-IT. "DO-IT HTML Guidelines for Web Pages." Document. Seattle: University of Washington, 1997.

———. "Making Library Resources Accessible to People with Disabilities." Document. Seattle: University of Washington, 1997.

———. *Universal Access: Electronic Resources in Libraries Presentation Materials.* Presentation kit assembled and edited by Sheryl Burgstahler, Dan Comden, and Beth Fraser. Seattle: DO-IT, 1997.

Earl, C. L., and J. D. Levanthal. "Windows 95—Access for Blind or Visually Impaired Persons: An Overview." *Journal of Visual Impairment and Blindness* 91 (September/October 1997): 5–9.

English, Wayne. "Multimedia PC and Accessibility." *Closing the Gap* (August/September 1997): 1–4.

Field, Peter, et al. "Review of Alternative Keyboards with Mouse Emulation with Netscape and Internet Explorer in the Macintosh or Windows 3.1 or 95 Environment." Diversity Management and the University of Toronto, Adaptive Technology Resource Centre (ATRC). January 7, 1997. Available at <www.utoronto.ca/atrc/reference/tech/altkeybd.html>.

Fraser, Beth. "DO-IT and the Libraries." *Library Directions* 7, no. 2 (Winter 1997). Available at <www.washington.edu/doit/Press.>

Gates, Bill. "Microsoft's Continued Commitment." Address given during "Accessibility Day '98." February 19, 1998. Available at <www.microsoft.com/enable/universal/default>.

———. "Helping People with Disabilities Helps Everyone." *New York Times,* August 13, 1997.

Gill, Kathy. "What Makes A Great Web Site?" eNetDigest, Review Criteria. Available at <www.enetdigest.com/design/review.html>.

Glossary of Adaptive Technologies: Screen Magnification. University of Toronto, Adaptive Technology Resource Centre (ATRC). Available at <www.utoronto.ca/atrcreference/tech/scmag.html>.

Gorman, Audrey J. "The 15% Solution: Kids with LD Can't Wait." *American Libraries* 28 (June-July 1997): 97–98.

Hendrix, Paul, and Michael Birkmire. "Adapting Web Browsers for Accessibility." Paper presented by Paul Hendrix, Center for Accessible Technology, and Michael Birkmire, Learning Independence through Computers, Inc., at the 1998 CSUN Conference sponsored by the University of California, Northridge, Center on Disabilities, March 1998. Available at <www.dinf.org/csun_98/csun98_113>.

Howell, Julie. "Good Design for Visually Impaired Users." (United Kingdom, Royal National Institute for the Blind) Informational page available at <www.RNIB.ORG.UK/wedo/research/access>.

———. "Hints for Designing Accessible Websites." (United Kingdom, Royal National Institute for the Blind) Informational page available at <www.RNIB.ORG.UK/wedo/research/hints>.

Jenkins, Phil. "Experience Implementing Web Accessibility Guidelines in IBM." IBM Special Needs Systems. Paper prepared by IBM Special Needs Systems. Available at <www.ibm.com/sns>.

Lazzaro, Joseph J. *Adaptive Technologies for Learning and Work Environments.* Chicago: American Library Association, 1993.

———. *Adapting PCs for Disabilities.* Reading, Mass.: Addison Wesley Longman, 1997.

Learning to Read: Reading to Learn: Helping Children with Learning Disabilities Succeed. Informational kit. Eugene, Ore.: National Center to Improve the Tools of Educators. Available at <www.indiana.edu/~eri_rec>.

Levanthal, J. D., and C. L. Earl. "A Review of Two Speech Access Programs for Windows 95; Slimware Window Bridge and WinVision." *Journal of Visual Impairment and Blindness* 92 (April 1998): 240–244.

Loy, Beth, and Linda C. Batiste. "Surfing the Net: The Three Keys to Universal Access." Presentation by Loy and Batiste of the Job Accommodation Network, West Virginia University. Available at <www.dinf.org/csun_98/csun98_011>.

Magical Mist Creations. "Making Your Site Speech Friendly." Posted October 1997. Available at <www.webit.com/magical/~mist/speech>.

McArthur, Laurie. "Adaptive Technologies: Alternative Keyboard Systems." *Technical Glossary.* Toronto: University of Toronto, Adaptive Technology Resource Centre (ATRC). Available at <www.utoronto.ca/atrc>.

McCall, Karen. "ZoomText Xtra-Beta, Evaluation." Toronto: University of Toronto, Adaptive Technology Resource Centre (ATRC). Available at <www.utoronto.ca/atrc/uiap/en/zoomtext>.

Melvin, Chuck. "His Master's Voice: Software Now Makes It Possible to Tell Your PC Exactly What You Want." *Plain Dealer* (January 19, 1998).

Microsoft Corp. "Microsoft Accessibility and Disabilities." *Legal Notices,* December 9, 1997. Available at <www.microsoft.com/enable/about>.

Mid-Hudson Library System. "Now That We've Met, What Do I Say? Guidelines for Communication with Persons Who Have Disabilities." New York: Mid-Hudson Library System, Outreach Services Department, 1994.

Murphy, Arthur R. "Design Considerations: Readers with Visual Impairments." Baltimore. Available at <www.lcc.gatech.edu/gallery/dzine/access>.

National Center for Accessible Media. "Web Access Symbol Now Available." Boston, Mass.: CPB/WGBH, 1997.

National Library Service. "Assistive Devices for Use with Personal Computers." Reference Circular. Compiled by Carol Strauss. Washington, D.C.: Library of Congress, 1997.

———. "Getting Started with Computers, Adaptive Equipment, and the Internet." Informational Brochure. Compiled by Judith Dixon (May 1998). Available at <lcweb.loc.gov/nls>.

Nguyen, Ken, and Linda Petty. "Web Browsing through Adaptive Technology: A Consumer Information Resource." Toronto: University of Toronto, Adaptive Technology Resource Centre (ATRC). Available at <www.toronto.ca/atrc/rd/llibrary/papers/access>.

The Orton Emeritus Series of monographs is published by the International Dyslexia Association. Each is dedicated to a specific topic. Information is available online at <www.interdys.org/bookstor.htm>.

"Adults with Dyslexia: Aspiring and Achieving" by Joan R. Knight.

"Basic Facts about Dyslexia, Part 1: What Every Layperson Ought to Know" by Angela Wilkins, Alice Garside, and Mary Lee Enfield.

"College: How Students with Dyslexia Can Maximize the Experience" by Joan Stoner, Mary Farrell, and Barbara Priddy Guyer.

"Doctors Ask Questions about Dyslexia: A Review of Medical Research" by Sylvia Richardson and Gordon F. Sherman.

"Independent Schools and Programs for Individuals with Dyslexia: What Are the Questions?" by Jean M. Foss and Diana Hanbury King.

"Justice for All" by James Oliver Antonoff and Karen Norlander.

"Kids Who Learn Differently: Strategies for Successful Learning" by Nancy Hennessy and Louise H. Rothschild.

"The Other Sixteen Hours: The Social and Emotional Problems of Dyslexia" by Michael Ryan.

"Phonological Awareness: A Critical Factor in Dyslexia" by Joseph Torgesen.

"Reading, Writing and Spelling: The Multisensory Structured Language Approach" by Helaine Schupack and Barbara A. Wilson.

"Testing: Critical Components for the Identification of Dyslexia" by Jane Fell Greene and Louisa Cook Moats.

Pierce, Kelley. "The Right Stuff: How to Choose Adaptive Technology." *Computer Users Network News: Adaptive Technology for the Blind and Visually Impaired* 3, no. 5 (March-September 1997). Online newsletter available at <www.city-net.com/vipace/friends/chicago>.

Porter, Lake. "Voice Recognition System," *Glossary of Adaptive Technologies: Voice Recognition.* Toronto: University of Toronto, Adaptive Technology Resource Centre (ATRC). Available at <www.utoronto.ca/atrc/tech/voicerecog>.

Shettle, Andrea. "Welcome to the Web." *Gallaudet Today* 27 (Spring 1997): 6–12.

Shumila, Dena, and Jan Richards. "Increasing Access to World-Wide Web Sites for Blind and Visually Impaired Computer Users." Toronto: University of Toronto, Adaptive Technology Resource Centre (ATRC). Available at <www.toronto.ca/atrc/rd/library/papers/access>.

Stone, Brad. "Are You Talking to Me?" *Newsweek* (March 2, 1998): 85–86.

Trace Center. "Universal Design, Principles and Guidelines." Madison, Wisc.: The Center. Available at <www.Trace.Wisc.edu/world/gen_ud>.

———. *Introduction to Assistive Rehabilitation Technologies.* InterAct Course Guide. Madison, Wis.: The Center, 1994.

———. *Trace Resourcebook: Assistive Technologies for Communication, Control and Computer Access.* Ed. Peter Borden, Jaime L. Lubich, and Gregg Vanderheiden. Madison, Wis.: The Center, 1996.

Treveranus, Jutta, and Chris Serflek. "Alternative Access to the World Wide Web." Toronto: University of Toronto, Adaptive Technology Resource Centre (ATRC). Available on <www.toronto.ca/atrc/rd/library/papers/access>.

United Cerebral Palsy Association. "National Leaders Support the Future of Assistive Technology for People with Disabilities." Washington, D.C., January 15, 1998. Available at <www.ucpa.org/html/whatsnew/atpress.html>.

University of Toronto. "Making Connections: A Guide for Library Staff Serving Persons with Disabilities." Toronto: University of Toronto, 1994.

Uslan, M. M., and J. C. Su. "A Review of Two Screen Magnification Programs for Windows 95: Magnum 95 and LP Windows." *Journal of Visual Impairment and Blindness* 91 (September-October 1997): 9–12.

Vanderheiden, G. C. "Unified Web Site Accessibility Guidelines Version 7.2." Madison, Wis.: Trace R&D Center, 1997. Available at <www.trace.wisc.edu/text/guide;ns/htmlgide>.

———. "A Standard Approach for Full Visual Annotation of Auditorially Presented Information for Users, Including Those Who Are Deaf: Showsounds." Madison, Wis.: Trace R&D Center, 1992.

Vogel, Susan A. "Teaching Suggestions for Adults with Suspected Learning Disabilities/Differences." *National Institute for Literacy Newsletter* 3, no. 4 (Spring 1996): 11.

Wakefield, Doug. "World Wide Web and Disabled People." Article presented for Center for Internet Technology Accommodation, General Services Administration. Available at <www.unik.no/~mortent/article/wwwdsbl/www_dsbl.html#ART1>.

Walker, Jasen M., and Fred Heffner. "In the Blink of an Eye: What Business Leaders Still Don't Understand about Disabilities." *In the Mainstream* 20, no. 2 (March/April 1995: 17–19).

"Web Content Accessibility Guidelines 1.0 W3C Recommendations 5 May 1999." Wendy Chisholm, Gregg Vanderheiden, and Ian Jacobs. Available at <www.w3.or/TR/1999/WAI-Webcontent>.

"Welfare Foundation Offers Sound Advice on Increasing Odds for Winning Grants." *Disability Funding News* (February 26, 1998): 9.

Resources for Continuing Education

Closing the Gap, Inc.
P.O. Box 68
Henderson, MN 56044
Voice: (507) 248-3294
Website: <www.closingthegap.com>.

Closing the Gap publishes an annual resource directory of adaptive hardware and software devices as well as a monthly newsletter. Topics are diversified and writing clear and comprehensive. There are often reviews of new products and tips for easier access to Windows and the Internet.

Disability Funding News
8294 Fenton Street
Silver Spring, MD 20910

Offers funding referrals and resources for grants that will aid persons with disabilities. Success tips are offered.

Envision
The Lighthouse Inc.
111 East 59th Street
New York, NY 10022

A quarterly publication of the Lighthouse National Center for Vision and Child Development, the newsletter may feature articles on choosing adaptive equipment, software, and information on the causes and solutions to some visual impairments.

Equal Access to Software and Information (EASI)

Online journal available free of charge from St. John's University's Project EASI. To subscribe, send an e-mail message to <listserv@ maelstrom. stjohns.edu> leaving the subject line blank. In the body of the message write "Sub itd-jnl YOUR FIRST NAME YOUR LAST NAME" or log on at <www.rit.edu/~easi/easi> to read as time permits.

Exceptional Parent Magazine
555 Kinderkamack Road
Oradell, NJ 07649
Website: <www.eparent.com>

Written in a parent-to-parent style, this magazine presents updates on new products and programs designed to help children with disabilities. Of exceptional value is its *Annual Resource Guide.*

Focus on Electronic Information
National Library Service for the Blind and Physically Handicapped

Library of Congress (NLS/BPH)
1291 Taylor Street, N.W.
Washington, DC 20542
<www.loc.gov/nls/reference/focus.html>

A monthly bulletin highlighting Websites that are useful to all, but the information found at the sites is not readily available in special media for those with print disabilities.

Focus: Library Service to Older Adults, Persons with Disabilities
Ruth O'Donnell, Editor
3509 Trillium Court
Tallahassee, Florida 32312-1716
<odonnellr@worldnett.att.net>

A chatty newsletter that succinctly alerts readers to new products, helpful Websites, and resources. *Focus* also encourages readers to share success stories and receive solutions to questions they ask.

Journal of Visual Impairment and Blindness
American Foundation for the Blind
11 Penn Plaza, Suite 300
New York, New York 10001

This journal reviews new products for the adapted access of information. The articles are written by research professionals employed by the American Foundation for the Blind. Also included are short news releases about products designed for use by people with visual impairments and a calendar of upcoming events.

MAINSTREAM and MAINSTREAM Online
2973 Beech Street, Suite I
San Diego, CA 92102
Online edition may be found at <www.mainstream-mag.com>.

MAINSTREAM is comprised of articles concerning disability rights, employment issues, travel, and general-interest features. Also included are listings and reviews of new products and technology. MAINSTREAM often offers information on the availability of grants for technology.

Tactic
Clovernook Center
7000 Hamilton Avenue
Cincinnati, Ohio 45231-5297

A consumer-oriented quarterly that focuses on adaptive technology with specific references to computer access. New products are reviewed; articles concern access to the Web.

Index

Barbara Mates is the head of the Cleveland Library for the Blind and Physically Handicapped, a part of the Cleveland Public Library. She is a speaker and writer on the subject of library services to persons with visual and physical disabilities and has written a previous book and numerous articles on the subject. Mates advocates finding the correct balance of common sense, humanity, and technology to render library services to all persons. Past Chair of the Libraries Serving Special Populations Section (LSSPS) of the Association of Specialized and Cooperative Library Agencies (ASLCA), she also has chaired several committees and sections within ASCLA.

Judith M. Dixon is Consumer Relations Officer at the National Library Service for the Blind and Physically Handicapped, Library of Congress, which provides Braille and recorded reading material to blind and physically handicapped Americans. She holds a Ph.D. in clinical psychology from Adelphi University (1980).

Doug Wakefield is an accessibility specialist with the U.S. Access Board, where he is the lead staff person in the development of functional and performance standards for information technology to implement the requirements of the new 508 amendment to the Rehabilitation Act. He also is the Board's telecommunications access specialist.